everyday epicurean

simple, stylish recipes
for the home chef

Catherine Bell

photographs by
Kieran Scott

TEN SPEED PRESS
Berkeley • Toronto

First published in 1999 by
TANDEM PRESS, New Zealand

TEN SPEED PRESS
PO Box 7123
Berkeley, California 94707
www.tenspeed.com

Distributed in Canada by
Ten Speed Press Canada

Design by Christine Hansen

Library of Congress
Cataloging-in-Publication
Data is on file with the publisher

ISBN 1-58008-225-4

First U.S. printing, 2000
Printing in Hong Kong by
South China Printing Co.

1 2 3 4 5 6 7 8 9 10 — 02 01 00

contents

preface

In 1984 I was in London, studying at Leith's School of Food and Wine, hoping to fine tune my skills as a cook. Even then it was an expensive place to live and so on Saturdays I worked, earning the amazing sum of $30, at Divertimenti – the fabulous cookware store on Fulham Road. The money, barely enough, was supplemented by the odd dinner party or a weekend cooking at a country house. Slave labor when I think back. However, my time at Divertimenti stood me in good stead when I opened the Epicurean five years later. In between, I had cut my teeth on a delicatessen, opening Auckland's first seven-day speciality food store, producing everything onsite and importing unusual ingredients such as Arborio rice and balsamic vinegar! It was during this time that the concept of a cookware store, combined with a cooking school, started to form.

Now, 10 years later, we can't keep up. Classes fill within days of our schedules being delivered. Customers up and down the country are able to access our products by mail order and the Internet. The challenge to find new ideas and new products has increased, taking me abroad each year to trade shows and conferences, and to study other retail concepts and explore what's happening with food.

Initially, when the cookschool was established, it was a place where chefs from well-known restaurants could showcase their dishes to those wanting to emulate them in their own kitchens at home or simply enjoy watching a master at work. It was theater, a form of entertainment for some and a serious learning experience for others.

Over the years, as demand has grown and as people's interest in food has changed, our classes have evolved. Dishes are much more approachable for the home cook, although no less inspiring. On the whole, they need to be fast to prepare and take into account the changing attitudes to healthy eating, without taking away the enjoyment of good food.

I remember my nerves the day I taught my first class, late in that first year. I introduced the 'students' to focaccia, risotto and panforte. They loved it and I was hooked, not just on teaching, but on inspiring and introducing people to new dishes, ingredients and methods.

A few years later, in 1993, on a visit to the USA, I taught a class at a little school outside San Francisco. In itself a worthwhile experience, it also gave me a valuable germ of an idea. The owner of that cookschool ran a class every week for just one hour, charged one dollar and took no reservations. It attracted people to her school as well as to her small cookware store. Well, any retailer is always looking for ways to bring more customers through the door. And so, in the very next schedule of classes a few months later, we began 'Gourmet on the Run', a one hour class, no reservation required, although we did charge a little more than a dollar. It didn't take long for word to travel. Very soon we were holding two a week to accommodate the rapidly rising numbers and since last year our Saturday morning classes have been bringing many new faces to the school.

In 'Gourmet on the Run' we taste, we share experiences and opinions, but above all we enjoy food. This book is a collection of the very best fresh and fast dishes from these classes.

It enables me to share with you my passion for good, simple food and inspire you to prepare meals using fresh seasonal produce and incorporating a variety of styles and cuisines. I introduce you to new ingredients, tempt you, I hope, to cook more spontaneously and encourage you to see food and the preparation of it as a form of enjoyment, rather than a chore.

acknowledgements

there are many people without whom I would not have achieved my dream at Epicurean. They have encouraged, listened to and supported me prior to and during the last 10 years.

My mother, Robin, who, although she has not been here for 25 years, most definitely sowed the seed that eventually took me down the path as a cook. I'm very fortunate that her passion for good food rubbed off on me.

My father, Bill, from whom I'm fairly sure I inherited the desire to work for myself and the ambition to do 'my own thing'.

Tom and Olivia, who would love to have a mother who stays at home, but who, I'm pleased to say, have developed an excellent appreciation of food.

My past and present staff at Epicurean, especially Susan, Teresa, Helena and Judith, who have kept the cookstore running smoothly as I devote time to this project and others, and Jacqueline and Claire for sharing the load within the cooking school, and for their contribution to the recipe testing, proofreading and photographing for this book.

Our customers, without whom I would not be in business. There are many who I can count as true friends.

Allyson Gofton, who helped to get the cookschool off the ground in 1989 and for her willingness to share and advise over the years.

Bob Ross and Helen Benton at Tandem Press for seeing the potential in this book.

Kieran Scott for his magnificent photography that so truly reflects the Epicurean.

Christine Hansen for her design.

Alison Mudford for her editing skills, and Sara Haddad for coordinating production.

The many cooks, authors, chefs and restaurants who have inspired the recipes within this book. These have been gathered over a six-year period, and I am very aware that, having failed to keep appropriate records, we are unable to give credit where it is due to many of the recipes.

introduction

everyday Epicurean is intended to inspire you to cook fresh, flavorful food that does not need hours of preparation. However, in order to cook quickly or spontaneously, but without the use of prepared or value-added products, you need to think ahead, or have a few basic ingredients in the pantry. In today's world, few of us have the luxury of being able to shop daily but if, for instance, you have Arborio rice or egg noodles in the cupboard and homemade stock in the freezer, you have the makings of a risotto or a quick and nourishing noodle soup. On the way home, stop by the farmers market for a seasonal vegetable or the Asian store for a piece of barbecue pork, and dinner that night will be on the table in well under an hour and delicious too.

The ingredients used throughout the book run the gamut of the seasons and it is my hope that you will, for example, cook the asparagus dishes in the spring and early summer when the locally grown product is abundant and leave the imported stuff, available in the middle of winter, for the restaurants. One of life's pleasures is the first mouthful of foods such as asparagus or strawberries when you have not tasted them for six or nine months. It's what makes food exciting.

You will find the recipes in this book loosely grouped by type, e.g. soups or pasta. Many of the dishes can be utilized in several ways, for instance the Chinese Noodle Salad on page 137 could be a first course, a luncheon dish or part of a series of dishes at a barbecue or buffet. I have endeavored where appropriate to give suitable accompaniments and options. Basic recipes can be found as part of the glossary, where ingredients, methods and techniques are explained in more detail.

Try not to be bound by what you read. If a dish calls for basil but you have none, maybe parsley will work just as well. Perhaps lamb can be replaced with chicken or even fish. An asparagus risotto can easily become a pumpkin and spinach one and, if you don't like too much chile, reduce the quantity or even leave it out. There is almost always an alternative that will work – let your instincts guide you.

The only exception, of course, is with the baking of cakes or desserts, where measurements must be adhered to if the recipe is to be successful. I can't stress enough the importance of accurate measuring tools. Ideally, every kitchen should have a set of scales, measuring spoons and cups and a measuring pitcher for liquids.

Cooking is about many things, not just the body's need to eat. Is it idealistic to hope that we will never lose the ability to cook or the desire to share food around the table with family or friends?

Good cooking everyone!

the basic kitchen

In addition to the usual pots, pans, bowls and utensils, there are many gadgets and pieces of equipment that will make cooking far more efficient and enjoyable. When buying major pieces of equipment such as saucepans, knives or a food processor, I advise you to do your homework first, then purchase the best you can afford.

   Listed below are the essentials any cook needs to produce a wide range of dishes. It may seem a long list, but these things can be acquired gradually as the need arises. You may be surprised just how many you have already.

Pot & Pans
3 x saucepans, 14 cm, 16 cm & 18 cm
   (5$\frac{1}{2}$", 6$\frac{1}{2}$", 7")
1 x 20 cm (8") saucepan, either with one long
   handle or two handles
1 x stockpot, 8-10 liters (16-20 pints)
2 x frying pans, 24 cm & 28 cm (9$\frac{1}{2}$" x 11")
1 x roasting pan & rack
1 x ovenproof casserole

Utensils
Set of four mixing bowls
Measuring spoons
Measuring cups, $\frac{1}{4}$, $\frac{1}{3}$, $\frac{1}{2}$ & 1 cup
Measuring pitcher, 1 liter (2 pint) capacity with
   graduated markings
Meat thermometer
Metal utensils – fish slice, slotted spoon, fork, large
   spoon, ladle, potato masher
Four-sided grater
Wire whisk
Bottle opener
Can opener
Corkscrew
Lemon squeezer

2-3 wooden spoons
2 x rubber spatulas, preferably heat resistant
Colander
2 x wire-mesh sieves, large & small
Egg beater
Tongs
Vegetable peeler
Pepper grinder
Chopping board
Garlic press

Knives
10 cm (4") paring knife
15 cm (6") utility knife
20-23 cm (8-10") cook's knife
Bread knife
Sharpening steel

Baking Equipment
Baking sheets
Rolling pin
Cooling rack
Pastry brush
Teflon sheet
Variety of baking pans for cakes, muffins, tarts, loaves

Electrical Equipment
Set of scales, with metric and U.S. measurements
Hand blender or cake mixer
Food processor

Optional extras – things I wouldn't be without
Benriner slicer – a very sharp Japanese slicer,
   adjustable and with three julienne blades.
Electric spice grinder – an inexpensive electric coffee
   grinder dedicated to the job.
Zester – a simple tool that strips the zest from citrus
   fruit.
Ridged cast-iron grill – for chargrilling indoors –
   available in many sizes and shapes.
Bamix food machine – a wand mixer – blends soup
   in the saucepan.
Pressure cooker – long-cooked casseroles and soups

or freshly cooked beans can be achieved in a fraction of the time.

Ice-cream machine – small, relatively inexpensive machines to make smooth, creamy ice-creams, sorbets, frozen yogurts.

Pasta machine – a hand-rolling machine that clamps to the counter.

Salad spinner – dries salad leaves easily and efficiently.

Simmer mat – if you cook on gas, one of these will enable you to cook at a really low heat.

Wok – no kitchen should be without one. Essential for Asian stirfries, steaming, deep frying.

Stainless steel dough scraper – for scooping up chopped vegetables or herbs.

Bamboo steamer with two layers – can be used to steam anything.

Candy thermometer – use for deep frying and preserving.

Spraypump olive oil mister – gives a fine spray of your chosen olive oil, saves using a pastry brush to oil vegetables, meat or grill pans.

Garlic peeler – a flexible tube that peels garlic with one roll under the hand.

credits

I would like to thank the following companies for allowing me to use their products in the photographs within this book. Any product not noted is available at the Epicurean or is privately owned.

Acland Holdings (09) 373 5255 pages 21, 45, 65, 90, 123

Country Road Homewares Auckland (09) 638 8332 pages 45, 61, 93, 108, 113, 136

Domestic Agencies (09) 525 0127 pages 15, 50, 41

Peter Gower Ltd (09) 379 4708 pages 41, 67, 72, 93, 119, 141

Linden Row (09) 366 6040 pages 139, 176

Maytime Marketing (09) 526 4274 pages 33, 35, 136, 176

Nest (09) 445 3201 page 84

Parnell Agencies (04) 232 7709 pages 45, 48, 67, 99, 148, 160, 162

small bites

spinach and feta eccles

When you need to prepare lots of small bites, it pays to have one or two that can be done ahead and frozen. These pastries don't even need to be thawed before baking.

Sift the flour and salt into a bowl. Rub in the cream cheese and butter, and add enough iced water to form a firm dough. Form into a flat disc, wrap in plastic wrap and refrigerate for 30 minutes. The mixing can also be done in a food processor.

Heat the oil in a sauté pan and gently fry the garlic, spinach and green onions for 3-4 minutes. Remove from the heat and stir in the cheese and nuts; cool completely.

Divide the pastry in half and roll each portion into a 25 x 20 cm (10" x 8") rectangle. Spread the filling evenly over one of the rectangles and lay the other on top. Gently roll out together until the filling is just visible. Cut into rounds with a 6 cm (2½") cutter and place on a greased oven tray. Cut three small slits on the surface of each round and brush the tops with beaten egg.

Bake at 180°C/350°F for 15-20 minutes. Cool on a wire rack.

MAKES ABOUT 16.

Note: if you plan to freeze these, don't apply the egg wash until the time comes to bake them.

PASTRY

2 cups plain flour

pinch of salt

125 g (4½ oz) cream cheese

45 g (1½ oz) unsalted butter

ice-cold water

FILLING

2 teaspoons olive oil

1 clove garlic, chopped

250 g (8½ oz) spinach, stalks removed, washed well and finely shredded

4 green onions, finely chopped

150 g (5½ oz) feta cheese, crumbled

½ cup brazil nuts, finely chopped

1 egg, beaten

crostini di fegatini

Crostini make great pre-dinner snacks. Add to a salad and you have a first course or lunch dish. I can't stress enough the importance of fresh livers – frozen ones will alter the texture completely.

Clean the livers and remove any membrane.

Heat the butter and olive oil in a skillet over a medium heat and sauté the garlic and chicken livers until the livers are brown on the outside and still pink and juicy in the middle – about 4-6 minutes.

Add the wine and sage and cook for 1-2 minutes. Transfer to a food processor, add the other ingredients and process until smooth. Season to taste.

Spread on freshly grilled crostini and serve immediately.

MAKES ABOUT 1½ CUPS.

500 g (1 lb) fresh chicken livers

2 tablespoons unsalted butter

¼ cup extra virgin olive oil

3 cloves garlic, crushed

½ cup dry Marsala or dry white wine

a few sage leaves, chopped finely

5 anchovy fillets

3 tablespoons capers

freshly ground black pepper

crostini (see page 192)

crostini piccanti

Irresistible!

Place the bread on a plate and drizzle with the red wine vinegar. Leave for 10-15 minutes.

Squeeze the bread with your hands to remove any excess vinegar. Discard the vinegar and place the bread in the bowl of a food processor with the other ingredients. Process to a fine paste.

Spread on crostini and serve, sprinkled with a few extra pinenuts.

Will store, covered, in the fridge for 2-3 days.

MAKES ABOUT 1½ CUPS.

2 large slices country style bread, cut
   2½ cm (1") thick, crusts removed

3 tablespoons red wine vinegar

4 hardboiled egg yolks

6 anchovy fillets

3 tablespoons flat-leaf parsley

3 cloves garlic, roughly chopped

¾ cup pinenuts

4 teaspoons capers, drained and rinsed

12 large green olives, pitted

½ cup olive oil

salt and freshly ground black pepper

extra pinenuts to garnish

rosemary-scented white bean purée

Cannellini beans are available at speciality food stores, but you can use any small white bean such as haricot or lima for this purée. If you're using dried white beans, soak them overnight in cold water, drain and cook in fresh water until tender. A pressure cooker will shorten the cooking time considerably.

Combine the oil, garlic and rosemary in a medium pan and sauté for 5 minutes. The garlic should color very slightly.

Add the beans, plenty of salt and pepper and stir. Cook for approximately 10 minutes, adding some of the bean liquid if the mixture begins to dry out. Mash the beans to a rough purée, or, if you prefer a smoother texture, blend in the food processor. Taste and add lemon juice, salt and pepper as desired.

To serve, spread the bean purée onto grilled bread that has been rubbed with garlic and drizzle with a little more olive oil.

MAKES APPROXIMATELY 2 CUPS.

3 tablespoons extra virgin olive oil, plus extra for drizzling

3 garlic cloves, finely chopped

2 sprigs rosemary

2 cups cooked cannellini beans, cooking liquid reserved

salt and freshly ground black pepper to taste

juice of 1 lemon or to taste

salsa agresto

One of the highlights of 1997 was a week spent in Tuscany with my two gurus, Australian chefs Maggie Beer and Stephanie Alexander. This salsa is just one of the many wonderful dishes we prepared that week and ate at a long-table lunch each day, outside under the trees. Verjuice is the juice of unripe green grapes (see page 197). Its subtle acidity is quite unique, but substitute white wine if it proves elusive.

Preheat the oven to 220°C/425°F.

Roast the almonds and walnuts separately on a baking tray for about 5 minutes, shaking the trays to prevent the nuts from burning. Rub the walnuts in a clean tea towel to remove the bitter skins. Allow the nuts to cool.

Blend the nuts, garlic, herbs and seasonings with a little olive oil in a food processor to make a fine paste. Blend in the balance of the olive oil, then add the verjuice. The consistency should be perfect for using on crostini. If required, thin it a little with more verjuice.

MAKES ABOUT 2 CUPS.

1 cup whole almonds

1 cup fresh walnuts

2 cloves garlic

2³⁄₄ cups flat-leaf parsley

¹⁄₂ cup basil

1¹⁄₂ teaspoons salt

freshly ground black pepper

³⁄₄ cup extra virgin olive oil

³⁄₄ cup verjuice

Mahammara Pureé (left) and Salsa Agresto (right)

lentil tapenade

Although any kind of brown or green lentil will do, I find any excuse to cook lentilles de Puy, a smooth green lentil of exceptional quality, from France. A word of warning about commercial chicken stock (which probably has added salt). Be sure to dilute it with water by at least half and taste before salting the finished tapenade.

drain and rinse the lentils. In a large saucepan over a medium heat combine the lentils, stock, garlic and tomatoes. Simmer until the lentils are cooked, 30-45 minutes, adding more chicken stock if the pan starts to dry out. Set aside to cool.

Place all the ingredients from the saucepan in a food processor and process for 30 seconds, scraping down the sides several times. Add the oil, anchovies, capers, olives, lemon juice, salt and pepper to taste. Process until smooth. Add the parsley and pulse several times to blend.

Serve with toasted French bread or pita bread.

MAKES ABOUT 2 CUPS.

1 cup brown or green lentils

2$\frac{1}{2}$ cups chicken stock (see page 196), more if required

6 large garlic cloves, finely chopped

2 tablespoons sundried tomatoes, cut into slivers

1-2 tablespoons olive oil

2-4 anchovy fillets

3 tablespoons capers, drained

$\frac{1}{2}$ cup Kalamata olives, pitted

2 tablespoons fresh lemon juice

salt and freshly ground black pepper

$\frac{1}{2}$ cup flat-leaf parsley, finely chopped

muhammara purée

The flavour of bell peppers is greatly enhanced by roasting or grilling. Resist the temptation to rinse them under the tap while peeling – it only washes away the flavor. This purée also makes a delicious sauce for simple grilled chicken, lamb or fish.

Preheat the oven to 250°C/475°F.

Halve and seed the bell peppers. Brush with olive oil and sprinkle ⅔ of the garlic over the inside cavity. Roast the peppers for about 30 minutes, turning occasionally, until they start to crumple and soften. Remove from the oven and leave until cool enough to handle, then peel and slice.

Put the remaining garlic into a food processor with the peppers, walnuts, breadcrumbs, sugar, cumin, chile flakes, salt, lemon juice and pepper to taste. Blend at full speed until you have a smooth purée. Continue to process and slowly add the remaining oil. If it is still too thick, add a little more oil and a spoonful of water. Taste and add more salt and pepper if it is too bland. Spread onto a serving dish, pour over a little more oil and scatter over some minced chives.

Serve with warmed pita bread.

MAKES 1½ CUPS.

2 large red bell peppers
125 ml (½ cup) olive oil
3 cloves garlic, finely chopped
⅓ cup (40 g) walnuts, roasted and finely chopped
¾ cup (40 g) fresh white breadcrumbs
1 teaspoon sugar
1 teaspoon ground cumin
½ teaspoon hot chile flakes
½ teaspoon salt
juice of 1 lemon
pepper
chives to garnish

eggplant caviar

Make the most of eggplants when they are at their cheapest at the end of summer. A visit to my local market at Avondale will often yield as many as eight different varieties of all shapes, sizes and colors. The Mediterranean flavors in this paté make it an ideal addition to an antipasto platter or as a condiment to serve with barbecued lamb. Don't be tempted to leave the anchovies out, as they add an indefinable flavor.

Preheat the oven to 200°C/400°F.

Place the eggplant in a roasting pan and bake for about 30 minutes until the skin is blackened and the flesh soft. For a faster alternative, grill directly over a gas flame. Allow to cool a little, then peel off the charred skin.

Place the flesh into a food processor with the garlic, shallots, capers, anchovies, flat-leaf parsley and olive oil. Blend until smooth and season to taste with lemon juice, salt and pepper.

MAKES 1½ CUPS.

500-750 g (1-1½ lb) purple eggplant

3 large cloves garlic, chopped

3 shallots, finely chopped

1½ tablespoons capers, drained and chopped

5 anchovy fillets, mashed

3 tablespoons flat-leaf parsley, chopped

1 tablespoon extra virgin olive oil

2-3 tablespoons lemon juice

sea salt and freshly ground black pepper

feta and blue cheese spread

This is one of those ultra easy things that is good to have in the fridge as snack food or when friends pop in for a drink.

Combine all the ingredients in a bowl and mash with a fork. For a smoother consistency, blend in the food processor.

Serve with crusty bread or as part of a cheese platter.

Store, sealed in a jar, covered with a film of olive oil. Keeps in the refrigerator for up to 2 weeks.

MAKES 2½ CUPS.

400 g (14 oz) feta cheese

50 g (1¾ oz) strong blue-vein cheese, crumbled

¼ cup natural yogurt

¼ cup olive oil

2 teaspoons fresh oregano, chopped

1 small fresh chile, chopped (optional)

Dukkah is one of those age-old foods that has been rediscovered by the western world and popularized to the point where it can now be purchased ready-made in a supermarket. With their origins in the deserts of North Africa, these intriguing blends of spices, nuts and seeds can be stored for weeks, making an instant appetizer before a meal, along with good olive oil and flat bread for dipping.

dukkah

I was first introduced to dukkah by Middle Eastern food authority Claudia Roden, when she visited New Zealand. This is the one her mother made when Claudia was a child growing up in Cairo.

Toast the spices separately in a hot, dry pan over a medium heat until they are fragrant and just beginning to darken. Toast the nuts and sesame seeds on a baking tray in a hot oven until golden. Rub the hazelnuts in a teatowel to remove the skins.

Pound them together until they are finely crushed but not pulverized. If pulverized, the oils from the too finely ground seeds and nuts will form a paste.

Dukkah should always be a crushed dry mixture and definitely not a paste. Store in a sealed glass jar.

125 g (1$\frac{3}{4}$ cups) cilantro seeds

60 g ($\frac{1}{2}$ cup) ground cumin

60 g ($\frac{1}{2}$ cup) hazelnuts

250 g (2 cups) sesame seeds

sea salt and pepper to taste – try $\frac{1}{2}$ teaspoon salt and $\frac{1}{4}$ teaspoon pepper

MAKES APPROXIMATELY 4 CUPS.

bedouin spice blend

Although not strictly a dukkah without the addition of nuts, I discovered this mixture in one of my favorite books, Flatbreads and Flavors, *and use it in the same way as dukkah. It can also be mixed to a paste with olive oil and used to flavor soups and stews or as a marinade or rub.*

Toast the peppercorns, caraway and cardamom seeds separately in a dry skillet over a high heat for 2-3 minutes or until fragrant, stirring constantly. Combine and pound to a powder in a mortar and pestle or grind in a spice mill.

Toast the saffron in a dry pan over a medium heat until crisp. Add to the spices and pound or grind. Transfer to a bowl, add the turmeric and mix well. Store in a sealed glass jar.

2 tablespoons black peppercorns

1 tablespoon caraway seeds

$\frac{1}{2}$ teaspoon cardamom seeds

1 teaspoon saffron threads

1 teaspoon turmeric

MAKES APPROXIMATELY $\frac{1}{3}$ CUP.

herb fritters

Somehow I don't feel like I'm eating deep-fried food when I pop one of these delicious little morsels into my mouth. Serve them with drinks or use them as a simple garnish.

beat the egg yolks, then slowly add the oil, beer and flour. Season with salt and pepper to taste. Cover and set aside for 1 hour. Just before using, whisk the egg whites and fold into the batter. Thin if required with a little milk or water.

Wash the herbs and dry very well.

Place the olive oil in a frying pan to a depth of 1½ cm (½″). Heat until very hot but not smoking.

Dip the herbs into the batter one by one, shaking off any excess. Fry until crisp and golden. Drain and serve immediately, sprinkled with salt and garnished with lemon wedges.

2 eggs, separated

2 tablespoons olive oil

¾ cup beer

1 cup flour

salt and freshly ground black pepper

selection of fresh herb sprigs – basil, mint, sage, flat-leaf parsley

olive oil for frying

salt

lemon wedges

mini chicken and scallop fritters

Little fritters like these are an easy first course or hors d'oeuvre. The filling can be changed to include other vegetables, meat or shellfish, depending on what's available at the time. Serve the Spicy Gazpacho Sauce with barbecued meats or fish or over grilled vegetables.

Place the onion, peppers, zucchini and chives in a large bowl and mix well. Add the chicken meat, scallops, mayonnaise, eggs and breadcrumbs and blend well together. Put the mixture aside for 10-15 minutes to let the flavors meld.

Heat a little olive oil in a medium frypan and when hot add small spoonfuls of mixture. Fry on both sides until golden. Drain on paper towels. Serve with the Spicy Gazpacho Sauce for dipping.

MAKES 2-3 DOZEN.

100 g (3$\frac{1}{2}$ oz) onion, finely diced

100 g (3$\frac{1}{2}$ oz) each red and green bell pepper, finely sliced

100 g (3$\frac{1}{2}$ oz) yellow or green zucchini, finely sliced

$\frac{1}{4}$ bunch of chives, chopped

80 g (2$\frac{3}{4}$ oz) chicken meat, preferably breast, finely diced

80 g (2$\frac{3}{4}$ oz) fresh scallops, diced

100 g (3$\frac{1}{2}$ oz) mild mayonnaise

2 eggs

50 g (1 oz) fresh white breadcrumbs

olive oil for frying

spicy gazpacho sauce

Place all the ingredients, except the olive oil, in a blender and purée. With the blender still running pour the olive oil slowly into the sauce until it has a light shine to it.

Strain the sauce through a fine sieve if a smooth sauce is preferred. Taste and season with additional Tabasco if more spice is required.

Serve in a bowl alongside the fritters.

MAKES 2 CUPS.

1 large ripe tomato, cored and chopped

100 g (3$\frac{1}{2}$ oz) red bell pepper, chopped

100 g (3$\frac{1}{2}$ oz) cucumber, peeled and chopped

4 teaspoons (20 ml) red wine vinegar

1 clove garlic

salt and pepper

Tabasco sauce to taste

1 small fresh chile – optional

200 ml (7 fl oz) olive oil

baked turkish manti

Peter Chichester, one of the many chefs who teaches regularly at the Epicurean cooked these 'ravioli' at one of his classes. They are so irresistible we pinched the recipe to teach in 'Gourmet on the Run'. Fresh wonton wrappers can be found at any Asian market. What you don't use can be frozen.

Preheat the oven to 200°C/400°F.

In a mixing bowl combine all the ingredients well.

Place a small amount of mixture in the corner of each wonton wrapper. Brush the edges of pastry with egg wash and fold the corner over to make a rough triangle. Seal well and place on a greased baking sheet. Brush lightly with olive oil. Bake in a hot oven for 6-10 minutes until golden and crisp.

Serve hot with minted yogurt sauce.

MAKES APPROXIMATELY 60.

400 g (14 oz) ground lamb

$\frac{1}{4}$ cup crumbled feta

$\frac{1}{2}$ teaspoon ground cilantro

1 clove garlic, crushed

1 teaspoon ground cloves

$\frac{1}{2}$ teaspoon each cinnamon and ground cumin

1 teaspoon each paprika and dried oregano

1 teaspoon sea salt

freshly ground black pepper

$\frac{1}{3}$ cup (50 g) pinenuts, toasted and chopped

2 tablespoons olive oil

about 60 small wonton wrappers

egg wash made from a beaten egg mixed with a little water

minted yogurt sauce

Mix ingredients together and set aside in refrigerator to let the flavors develop.

MAKES 2 CUPS.

500 ml (2 cups) thick natural yogurt

$\frac{1}{2}$-1 cup finely chopped mint

squeeze of lime or lemon juice

fresh spring rolls

Buying the ingredients for these rice paper rolls always gives me an excuse to have a good prowl around one of Auckland's many Asian stores. The fish sauce, rice noodles and rice papers needed here keep indefinitely, so you can always have them on hand.

Soak the noodles in hot water for 10 minutes. Drain the noodles well and chop into short lengths. Mix noodles with the chiles, fish sauce, lime juice and sugar.

Dip a sheet of rice paper in warm water and lay on a flat surface. Place 2 prawns on one side of the rice paper and then a heaped tablespoon of the mixture. Cover with about 6 basil leaves and a small piece of lettuce. Bring the ends of the rice paper together and roll up, enclosing the filling firmly. Arrange on lettuce leaves with the prawns showing through the top and the seam underneath.

Combine the sauce ingredients, stirring to dissolve the sugar.

Garnish with fine shreds of carrot, daikon radish or green onion. Serve the sauce in a small bowl for dipping.

MAKES 8 ROLLS.

1 cup fine rice noodles

1 or 2 sliced chiles

2 teaspoons fish sauce

1 teaspoon lime juice or vinegar

1 teaspoon sugar

8 rice paper sheets

16 small cooked prawns, shelled and
  deveined

a few fresh basil leaves

soft lettuce leaves

shredded carrot, white radish and
  green onions

DIPPING SAUCE

4 tablespoons sugar

$\frac{1}{2}$ cup cold water

2 tablespoons fish sauce

finely sliced red and green chile

1 tablespoon lime juice or vinegar

pakora with a spiced tomato chutney

Unlike the herb fritters on page 20, these pakora will hold and reheat successfully if done ahead. This recipe calls for whole individual vegetables, but you can also combine diced vegetables with the batter, and simply drop spoonfuls into the oil to form small 'fritters'.

Sieve the flour, salt and chile powder into a bowl. Stir in enough water to make a thick batter. Mix well until smooth and allow to stand for 30 minutes. Stir the garlic, ginger and chile into the batter, then add the melted butter.

Heat the oil in a deep pan. Drop the onion rings into the batter and coat well. Deep fry until crisp and golden brown. Remove from the pan with a slotted spoon and drain on paper towels. Keep warm.

Repeat this process with the other vegetables.

Serve warm with the fresh tomato chutney.

1 cup (125 g) chickpea flour

1 teaspoon salt

$\frac{1}{2}$ teaspoon chile powder

$\frac{2}{3}$ cup water, approximately

1 clove garlic, finely chopped

2$\frac{1}{2}$ cm (1") piece of ginger, finely chopped

1 green chile, finely chopped (optional)

1 teaspoon butter, melted

vegetable oil for deep frying

2 onions, cut into rings

8 small fresh spinach leaves

2-3 small potatoes, parboiled and sliced

tomato chutney

Heat the oil in a saucepan. Add the onion and cook until soft. Add the tomatoes, ginger, cumin, cilantro, chile powder and salt. Simmer uncovered until the mixture thickens.

Add water, chile and sugar and continue to cook for 10 minutes, or until fairly thick.

MAKES APPROXIMATELY 2 CUPS.

2 tablespoons olive oil

1 onion, finely chopped

6 large ripe tomatoes, chopped or 2 x 400 g (14 oz) cans of tomatoes in juice

2$\frac{1}{2}$ cm (1") piece of ginger, finely chopped

1 teaspoon ground cumin

1 teaspoon ground cilantro

$\frac{1}{2}$ teaspoon chile powder

1 teaspoon salt

$\frac{1}{2}$ cup water

3 green chiles, chopped (optional)

1 teaspoon brown sugar

eggplant and walnut rollups

I've often served these rollups on a big platter as part of a buffet, or on an antipasto plate. Served with a salad and some crusty bread, they make a perfect dish for an alfresco lunch.

Cut the stems off the eggplants and slice in half lengthways. Salt the cut sides liberally, place cut sides down on a board or cookie sheet, and press flat. The easiest method is to place a cutting board or a baking sheet on top, then top it with a heavy cast-iron pan. Let the eggplants stand for at least 1 hour or as long as 3 hours – you want them to be as flat as possible.

To make the filling, combine the walnuts, garlic, cilantro and fenugreek seeds, salt and chile in a food processor and process until a thick paste forms. Turn out into a bowl and stir in the remaining ingredients, except the oil. Stand at room temperature for 10-15 minutes to let flavors blend.

Rinse the salt from the eggplants and squeeze out the excess juices. Dry well.

Heat a large frying pan over a medium-high heat and add 1 tablespoon of the oil. When the oil is hot, add half the slices. Reduce the heat to medium, cover and steam cook for about 15 minutes until the skin is soft and the flesh is moist and greyish all through.

Spread a thick layer of the filling on the cut side of each slice, roll up and place on a serving platter, seam side down. Refrigerate before serving, to allow the filling to firm slightly. Serve garnished with tomato wedges, mint and basil leaves.

MAKES 12-14 ROLLS.

6-7 long thin Japanese eggplants

salt

tomato wedges, mint and basil leaves to garnish

FILLING

$\frac{3}{4}$ cup walnut pieces, lightly roasted

2-3 cloves garlic

1 teaspoon cilantro seeds, dry roasted and ground

$\frac{1}{4}$ teaspoon fenugreek seeds, briefly dry roasted and ground

$\frac{1}{2}$ teaspoon salt

pinch of dried chile flakes

handful fresh cilantro, chopped

handful fresh basil or mint leaves, chopped

2 large sprigs flat-leaf parsley, chopped

3 green onions, finely chopped

1 tablespoon lemon juice

1 teaspoon balsamic vinegar

2 tablespoons olive oil

breads

Flatbreads, leavened or not, are extremely easy to make and so good to eat straight from the oven. They rarely require the level of kneading normally associated with breadmaking. A pizza stone is a good investment if you enjoy making your own pizza and breads. It will add a wonderful flavour and give a crisp finish to the base. As an alternative though, simply preheat a heavy baking sheet or the flat side of a cast-iron griddle in the oven.

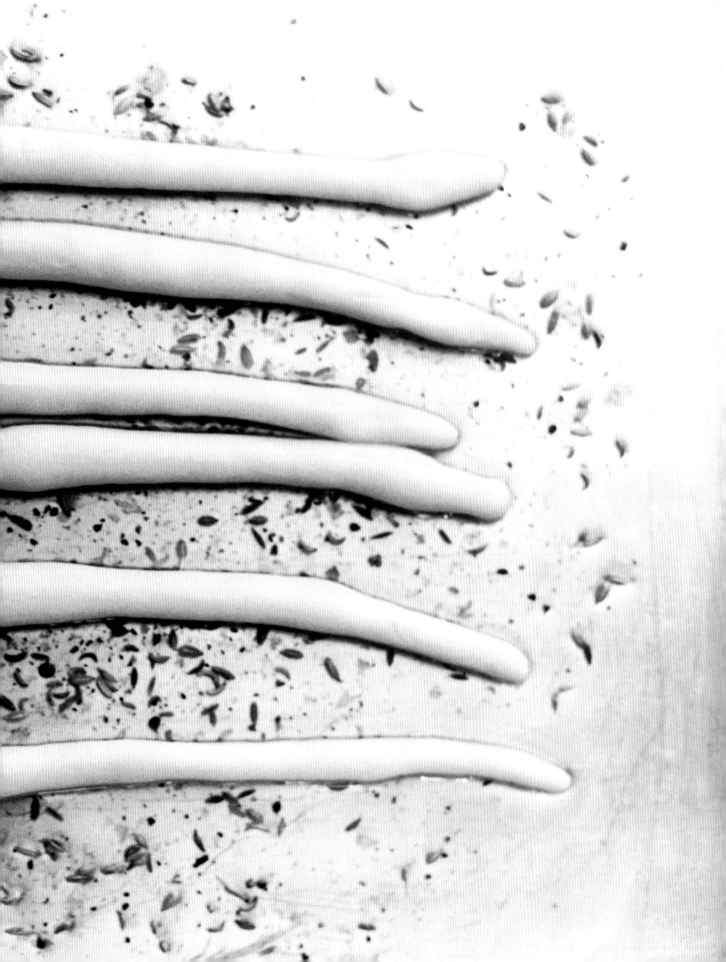

grissini

These bread sticks bear no resemblance to the grissini found in packets on the tables of bars and trattoria in Italy and elsewhere around the world. These are chewy, with a hint of fennel and salt and it is very hard to restrict consumption to just one or two. I first made them during my magical week in Tuscany with Maggie Beer and Stephanie Alexander.

Sprinkle the dried yeast over the water and leave until foaming. Place the flour and salt in a bowl. Make a well in the middle and pour in the honey, olive oil and yeast mixture. Combine and knead well until smooth. Put the dough into a lightly greased bowl, cover with a tea towel and allow it to stand in a draft-free spot until the dough has doubled in size – about 1 hour. Punch down gently. Allow the dough to double in size again – about 30 minutes.

Meanwhile, preheat the oven to 180°C/350°F. Break off small pieces of dough the size of a walnut and roll each into a thin sausage about 25 cm (10") long. Roll grissini in olive oil, fennel seed, crystal salt and pepper. Bake immediately, spaced well apart on a baking tray, for 15 minutes until browned and crisp. Remove from the oven and once again roll in the olive oil, salt and fennel seed mixture before cooling.

2 teaspoons active dried yeast

$\frac{1}{2}$ cup lukewarm water

2 cups flour

1 teaspoon sea salt

1 teaspoon honey

1 tablespoon extra virgin olive oil

extra olive oil, sea salt, pepper and fennel seeds

MAKES 2-4 DOZEN, DEPENDING ON SIZE.

carta da musica

With its origins in Sardinia, this bread has been popularized recently by food writers such as Claudia Roden. Peter Chichester introduced it at the Epicurean, brushing it with lavender infused olive oil. I enjoy it sprinkled with parmesan and sea salt as part of an antipasto-style plate.

Combine the flours and salt. Slowly add the water, mixing until a smooth dough is achieved. Knead slightly, form into a ball and rest for 10 minutes.

Place a pizza stone in the oven and preheat to 220°C/425°F.

Divide the dough into 10 balls and roll each out on a lightly floured surface until paper thin.

Brush liberally with olive oil and place on the pizza stone one at a time to bake. Turn and remove when crisp and golden.

Brush again with olive oil and sprinkle with Parmesan and salt. The bread can be cut into manageable sizes before baking or broken into jagged shards once baked.

MAKES 10.

2 cups flour
²⁄₃ cup (125 g) fine semolina flour
³⁄₄ teaspoon sea salt
200-350 ml (9-12 fl oz) water
extra virgin olive oil
freshly grated Parmesan cheese
sea salt

lavosh

These crisp, seeded breads are spectacular teamed with grissini or carta da musica in a bread basket. A pasta machine makes light work of the rolling and ensures that the dough is really thin.

Put the flour, sugar and salt into a food processor. Beat the egg and mix with the water and butter. With the motor running, slowly pour the liquid through the feed tube. As soon as the mixture forms a ball, stop the machine. Alternatively, knead by hand to a smooth elastic dough. Wrap in plastic and refrigerate for 1 hour.

Preheat the oven to 190°C/375°F.

Divide the dough into 6 balls. On a floured surface, roll each ball into a thin round, or pass between the rollers of a pasta machine until very thin. Place on greased baking sheets, brush with beaten egg and water, then sprinkle with seeds and coarse salt. Cut each round into 4 or 5 shards. Bake until pale gold and very crisp. If rolled by machine, they will need only 8-10 minutes. If rolled by hand, they will take a little longer. Cool on a wire rack and store in an airtight container.

MAKES 24-30.

2½ cups flour

1 teaspoon sugar

1 teaspoon sea salt

1 large egg

150 ml (5¼ fl oz) water

1 tablespoon melted butter

1 egg beaten and mixed with
* 2 tablespoons water*

2 tablespoons sesame seeds

1 tablespoon poppy seeds

1 teaspoon caraway seeds, optional

coarse salt for sprinkling

naan

Another flat bread, but this time a leavened one – just one of the many Indian breads used as a utensil to scoop up rice or curry and lift it to the mouth. Made ahead, they will reheat, wrapped, in a warm oven. They will also freeze successfully.

Sprinkle the yeast over the warm water in a large bowl. Stir to dissolve.

Place the yogurt in a medium bowl and gradually stir in the boiling water. Let cool to tepid.

Stir the yogurt mixture into the yeast mixture. Stir in 3 cups of flour, $\frac{1}{2}$ cup at a time. Then stir for 2 minutes in the same direction. Cover with plastic wrap and let stand for 30 minutes.

Sprinkle the oil and salt onto the yeast mixture. Mix in enough of the remaining flour, $\frac{1}{2}$ cup at a time, to form a dough. Turn out onto a lightly floured surface and knead until smooth and elastic, adding more flour if the dough is sticky – about 10 minutes.

Lightly oil the large bowl. Add the dough, turning to coat the entire surface. Cover with a damp kitchen towel or plastic wrap and let rise until doubled in volume – about 1 hour.

Place a pizza stone or baking tray in the center of the oven and heat to 230°C/450°F.

Punch the dough down and divide into 6 pieces. Using lightly floured hands, flatten each piece into an oval. Cover and let rest for 10 minutes.

Stretch or roll gently into a long oval, 20-25 cm (8-10") and lay on the pizza stone or baking tray, pressing down firmly.

Bake for 10-15 minutes, turning once, until the naan are puffy and brown. Wrap in foil or cloth to keep soft until ready to serve.

MAKES 6.

2 teaspoons active dry yeast

$\frac{1}{2}$ cup warm water

1 cup chilled plain unsweetened yogurt

1 cup boiling water

$6\frac{1}{2}$ cups flour

2 tablespoons vegetable oil

2 teaspoons salt

bulgur bread

The origin of this flatbread is of course Turkey, where it is just one of many breads made by the Kurds. Baked for a shorter time, the breads remain soft and pliable, or leave them in the oven for another minute and they will crisp up. Either way, they make a great addition to a mezze plate and are delicious eaten with dips or salsas.

In a medium-sized bowl, combine the bulgur, salt and onion. Pour the boiling water over and let stand for 30 minutes. Transfer to a food processor and process for about 20 seconds. Add 1 cup of flour and process to a smooth texture. Turn the mixture out onto a floured surface and knead, incorporating flour as necessary to keep dough from sticking. Cover the dough and let stand until you are ready to proceed further – from 15 minutes to 3 hours.

Place a baking stone or baking sheet in the oven and preheat to 230°C/450°F. Divide the dough into eight pieces and flatten each one on a well-floured surface. Roll dough out into very thin 20-15 cm (8-10") rounds (work with only as many as will fit in the oven at one time). Bake for $1\frac{1}{2}$-2 minutes, then turn and bake another minute or so until the edges begin to brown. Cook longer for crisper breads.

Keep breads warm by stacking and wrap in a clean kitchen towel.

MAKES 8.

2 cups bulgur wheat

1 teaspoon salt

$\frac{1}{2}$ cup onion, finely chopped or grated

2 cups boiling water

2 cups white flour, approximately

rosemary olive
oil bread

Ray McVinnie has taught many classes at the Epicurean and remains one of our most popular guest chefs. Although we have cooked many focaccia-style breads, this one, introduced to us by Ray, has always seemed the best. Lots of variations exist. Add any fresh herb you wish or a mixture of several, or incorporate olives or chopped green onions into the dough or roll it thin and use as a pizza base.

Sprinkle the yeast over the water and set it aside to work. Mix the flour, salt and rosemary together in a bowl and make a well in the center.

Mix the olive oil into the yeast mixture and pour into the flour. Mix well, kneading lightly to form a smooth dough. Place in an oiled bowl, cover and set aside to double in bulk (about 30 minutes).

Preheat the oven to 225°C/425°F. Grease a 28 cm (11") round pan with 3 tablespoons of olive oil or place a pizza stone in the oven to heat.

Punch down the dough. Push or roll the dough into a rough circle to fit the greased pan, or transfer to a floured pizza paddle. Paint the top liberally with olive oil, sprinkle with extra salt and dust the top with cornmeal. Slide onto the stone or place the pan in the oven. Bake for 20 minutes or until golden.

2 teaspoons active dried yeast

350 ml (12 fl oz) warm water

4 cups flour

1 tablespoon sea salt, plus extra

6 tablespoons extra virgin olive oil, plus extra

2-3 tablespoons fresh rosemary, finely chopped

coarse cornmeal

MAKES 1 LARGE LOAF.

fresh cilantro, ginger, and chile dosa

Although not a bread as we know it, these Indian 'dosa' or pancakes are eaten as a breakfast snack or as part of a meal to scoop up lentil and vegetable curries, such as the one on page 94. I have sometimes used this batter to make small crêpes, which I fold in four and serve on an Indian version of an antipasto platter, along with things such as pakora, tiny samosa and various dips.

Mix together the semolina flour, yogurt, chile, ginger, cilantro and salt. Stir in the water a little bit at a time until you have a smooth batter. Cover the bowl and let the batter rest for 1 hour.

Heat a heavy flat griddle over a medium-high heat. Using a paper towel, lightly oil the surface of the griddle and reserve the towel for use between each dosa.

When the griddle is hot, pour on $\frac{1}{2}$ cup of the batter. As you pour, move in a circle out from the middle, making as large a circle as possible; then use the back of a wooden spoon or a rubber spatula to spread the batter to cover the gaps. The pancake should be about 25 cm (10") in diameter. After about $1\frac{1}{2}$ minutes, begin to loosen then flip to the other side and cook for another 1-2 minutes.

If the batter is too thick, thin with a little more water.

MAKES 12-14 DOSA.

2 cups semolina flour

1 cup plain yogurt

1 red chile or jalapeño, seeded, veins removed and finely chopped

1 tablespoon finely chopped fresh ginger

2 tablespoons fresh cilantro, roughly chopped

$\frac{1}{2}$ teaspoon salt

2 cups warm water

soups

spring vegetable soup

As the weather warms up we tend to forget about soup as a meal option. This one, however, is a great way to take advantage of new spring produce. It's light and delicately flavored. Make sure the vegetables are just cooked, but should you overcook them, just purée the whole thing!

Melt the butter over a low heat in a large pot. Add the garlic and cook gently until fragrant. Add the tomatoes, stock, tarragon, salt and a good grind of pepper. Cover and cook for 30 minutes.

Meanwhile, cook the potatoes, carrots, radishes and asparagus separately in boiling water until just tender.

Purée the tomato mixture in batches and strain to remove any seeds. Return to the pot and add the milk.

Just before serving, reheat gently and, once hot, add all the vegetables, the basil and the dill.

Ladle the vegetables into shallow soup bowls and pour the soup around.

SERVES 8.

60 g (4 tablespoons) unsalted butter

6 large cloves garlic, finely chopped

2 kg (4½ lb) ripe tomatoes, coarsely chopped

3 cups chicken stock (see page 196)

2 teaspoons dried tarragon

1 teaspoon salt

freshly ground black pepper

8 small new potatoes

24 baby carrots

16-20 radishes, stems removed

12-16 spears asparagus, cut into 5 cm (2") lengths

1 cup milk

125 g (4½ oz) snow peas

12 basil leaves, cut into slivers

¼ cup fresh dill, chopped

chinese chicken soup

A simple, fragrant soup that makes a comforting one bowl meal after a busy day and another reason to keep a supply of chicken stock in the freezer. The rice noodles barely need cooking, making this an incredibly fast dish to prepare. Replace the oyster mushrooms with white or brown buttons if you wish.

bring the stock to the boil, reduce the heat and simmer gently.

In a food processor or blender, blend the garlic, green onions and ginger to a paste, adding a little of the oil if necessary.

Heat the oil in a wok until very hot, add the paste and stirfry for 1 minute, until fragrant. Add the chicken and stirfry with the paste for 1 minute.

Roughly chop the oyster mushrooms, Chinese leaves and sweetcorn. Add to the wok with the soy sauce and stirfry for another minute or so.

Pour in the stock, break in the rice noodles and stir. Simmer for a few minutes and add the cilantro leaves.

Season to taste and sprinkle over a few drops of sesame oil to finish.

SERVES 4-6.

2 liters (8 cups) chicken stock
  (see page 196)
2 garlic cloves
3 green onions
2½ cm (1") piece of fresh ginger
2 tablespoons vegetable oil
1-2 chicken breasts, skinned, boned
  and finely shredded
100 g (4 oz) small oyster mushrooms
1 bunch of Chinese greens, such as bok
  choy or choy sum
100 g (4 oz) canned or fresh baby
  sweetcorn
4 tablespoons soy sauce
100 g (4 oz) fine rice noodles
small bunch of cilantro, minced
salt and freshly ground black pepper
a few drops of sesame oil

laksa

Noodle dishes are almost overtaking pasta in popularity. Many of the Asian noodles just need to be covered in boiling water and left to soak, making them fast and effortless. Laksa, a fragrant Thai noodle soup, is exceptionally quick if you use a readymade laksa paste. If you do choose to make your own, make a larger quantity and freeze what you don't use.

Heat the oil in a wok, add the paste and fry over a medium heat until fragrant – about 3 minutes.

Add the stock and fish sauce. Add the chicken strips and simmer until tender. Add the coconut milk and bean sprouts, heat through gently, but do not boil or the sauce will curdle.

Cover the vermicelli with boiling water and soak until softened. Place the noodles into a bowl and pour hot soup over them. Garnish with cilantro, chile, green onions and lime juice.

SERVES 4-6.

3 tablespoons vegetable oil

$\frac{1}{2}$ cup laksa paste

3 cups chicken stock (see page 196)

1 tablespoon fish sauce

500 g (1 lb) chicken breast, cut into strips

420 ml (14 oz) can coconut milk

1 cup mung bean sprouts

100 g (4 oz) rice vermicelli, or any noodle of your choice

fresh cilantro to garnish

1 fresh red chile, for garnish

2 green onions, finely chopped for garnish

fresh lime juice

laksa paste

Seed the chiles and soak in boiling water.

Wrap the shrimp paste in foil and grill over a gas flame for a few minutes.

Peel the ginger and chop this and the lemongrass finely.

Place all the ingredients in a food processor and blend until fairly smooth. Add a little peanut oil to thin.

MAKES APPROXIMATELY $\frac{3}{4}$ CUP.

5 large dried red chiles

$\frac{3}{4}$ teaspoon shrimp paste

$\frac{1}{2}$ cup finely chopped shallots

5 cm (2″) piece of fresh ginger

2 stalks lemongrass (root end)

8 cloves garlic, finely chopped

$\frac{1}{2}$ teaspoon paprika

peanut oil to blend

vietnamese beef soup

The flavors of this soup are cleansing and satisfying. The easiest way to shave the beef so thinly is to partially freeze the fillet for an hour or so beforehand. The hot broth will cook the shaved beef instantly. Vietnamese mint is quite different to the English variety. It has a spicy, citrus taste and can be found at markets or Asian food stores, except during the colder months. It grows very well from cuttings, so pop a bit in a flower pot for a constant supply.

Simmer the broth ingredients, except the fish sauce, in a wok or large pot for 20 minutes. Strain, discarding the solids, and return the broth to the pan.

Add the fish sauce and reserve until needed.

Toss the shaved beef with the green onion and reserve.

Divide the bean sprouts, bok choy leaves, cilantro, Vietnamese mint, sliced chiles and lime quarters equally between 6 bowls. Pour a little hoisin and chile sauce into 6 small sauce bowls.

Bring the broth to a simmer.

Drop the rice noodles into boiling, salted water, drain immediately and toss with the peanut oil.

Divide the shaved beef and green onions into 6 portions and place in the bottom of 6 large, deep bowls.

Pour on the hot stock and add equal portions of noodles.

Serve immediately, accompanying each with a bowl of vegetables and sauce.

SERVES 6.

BROTH

2 liters (8 cups) beef stock
   (see page 196)

1 cinnamon stick

6 shallots, peeled and trimmed

8 cm (3") piece fresh ginger, sliced

2 stalks lemongrass, root end only,
   peeled and sliced

2 tablespoons fish sauce or to taste

TO FINISH

650 g (1$\frac{1}{2}$ lb) beef fillet in a piece,
   partially frozen, shaved very thin

6 green onions, sliced thinly

250 g (9 oz) bean sprouts

4 baby bok choy, leaves separated

$\frac{1}{2}$ cup cilantro

$\frac{1}{2}$ cup Vietnamese mint leaves

4 small red chiles, sliced thinly

2 limes, quartered

200 g (7 oz) rice noodles

salt

1 teaspoon peanut oil

hoisin sauce

chile sauce

cream of
roasted vegetable soup

Make this soup in autumn, using late summer bell peppers and eggplant and new season butternut pumpkin. Roasting caramelizes the sugars, intensifying the flavors. Using a mouli instead of the more modern food processor will eliminate the need to sieve the puréed vegetables to remove any skins or seeds.

Preheat the oven to 220°C/425°F.

Toss the vegetables and whole garlic cloves in olive oil in a large roasting pan and season with salt and pepper. Roast in the oven for about 30 minutes, or until the vegetables are quite tender and nicely browned, turning them often.

Meanwhile, melt the butter in a large pot over a low heat. Stir in the flour and cook for 1 minute. Whisk in the stock and simmer for 15 minutes.

When the vegetables are ready, squeeze out the roasted garlic and place in a food processor with the other roasted vegetables. Purée until smooth. Pass the purée through a sieve (only do this if you want a very smooth soup) and whisk in the stock. Simmer for 10 minutes. Add the cream and just heat through. Season to taste.

Garnish with fresh herbs and lemon zest or thinly sliced grilled garlic.

SERVES 4.

3 tablespoons olive oil

1 medium eggplant, cut into thick slices

500 g (1 lb) butternut pumpkin, peeled and cut into slices

2 large red bell peppers, cored and seeded

1 onion, quartered

6 cloves garlic, unpeeled

sea salt and freshly ground black pepper

2 tablespoons unsalted butter

$2\frac{1}{2}$ tablespoons plain flour

5 cups chicken stock (see page 196)

$\frac{1}{4}$-$\frac{1}{2}$ cup cream

fresh herbs and lemon zest to garnish

butternut, carrot
and cilantro soup

Even if you're not a fan of pumpkin soup, you will enjoy this variation. The carrot lightens it and the cilantro gives a delightful freshness. This soup freezes well, so make a double batch!

Preheat the oven to 190°C/375°F.

Place the butternut pieces on a baking sheet and bake until soft – about 30-40 minutes. When cooked, scrape the pulp from the skin and set aside.

Heat the olive oil in a large soup pot. Add the onion and sauté until soft. Add the paprika, cumin, turmeric, cilantro, salt and pepper, and sauté for 2 minutes. Add the butternut, carrot and sugar and cook for 10 minutes. Add the stock and water. Bring to a boil, reduce and simmer uncovered for 30 minutes or until the carrots are soft.

Allow to cool a little, then purée in a blender until the soup is very smooth. Taste and season with salt and pepper.

To serve, heat the soup and garnish with yogurt and fresh cilantro.

SERVES 4-6.

750 g (1 lb 10 oz) butternut pumpkin, seeded and cut into pieces

3 tablespoons olive oil

1 large onion, chopped

1 teaspoon paprika

1½ teaspoons ground cumin

¾ teaspoon turmeric

1 teaspoon ground cilantro

sea salt and freshly ground black pepper

4 carrots, peeled and coarsely chopped

1 teaspoon sugar

3 cups chicken stock (see page 196)

3 cups water

½ cup plain yogurt

2 tablespoons fresh cilantro, chopped

fishysoisse

We all voted this one of the most beautiful soups ever! The idea came from the book Canteen Cuisine *co-authored by Marco Pierre White and Michael Caine. We've enjoyed using our wonderful local hot-smoked fish. I particularly like my fishmonger's smoked orange roughy. It's moist and succulent and doesn't fall apart in the soup.*

Melt the butter in a large pot and sauté the leek and onion until soft but not colored. Add the potato, stock and water and cook for 10 minutes over a high heat.

Add the cream and cook a further 2 minutes. Remove half the vegetables and set aside. Purée the remaining soup. Put the solid vegetables back into the soup. Season to taste. Heat gently if required.

In a frypan combine the milk and water and gently poach the smoked fish for a few minutes only. Drain the fish and flake off into large pieces. Add to the soup along with the poaching liquid.

To serve, place the soup into bowls and sprinkle with the chives. Divide the fish between the bowls and serve immediately.

SERVES 6-8.

100 g (4 oz) unsalted butter

3-4 medium leeks, white part only, washed well and finely sliced

3 medium onions, finely sliced

3 medium potatoes, peeled and cut into medium sized dice

1$\frac{1}{2}$ liters (6 cups) chicken or fish stock (see page 196), boiling

250 ml (1 cup) water, boiling

200 ml (7 fl oz) cream

salt and freshly ground black pepper

300 ml (10 fl oz) milk and water mixed

225 g (8 oz) smoked fish, without skin or bones

fresh chives, finely chopped

potato-tomato soup
with rosemary

Rustic is the only word to describe this simple soup. How can such ordinary ingredients combine to make something so delicious? Floury, old potatoes work best.

Place the olive oil and onion in a soup pot and cook over a low heat until the onion is tender and golden. Add the tomatoes, rosemary and salt to taste. Simmer for 5 minutes.

Add the potatoes. Cook for 5 minutes. Add the water, bring to a boil, then adjust to a simmer. As the potatoes become tender, break them up with the back of a wooden spoon until a coarse purée forms.

Cook the soup for about 45 minutes or until thick.

Serve generously sprinkled with freshly grated Parmesan cheese.

SERVES 6.

4 tablespoons olive oil

1 small onion, finely diced

2 cups crushed tomatoes, canned
  or fresh

2 teaspoons finely chopped rosemary

sea salt to taste

3 medium potatoes, peeled and cut into
  small dice

2 cups water

freshly grated Parmesan cheese

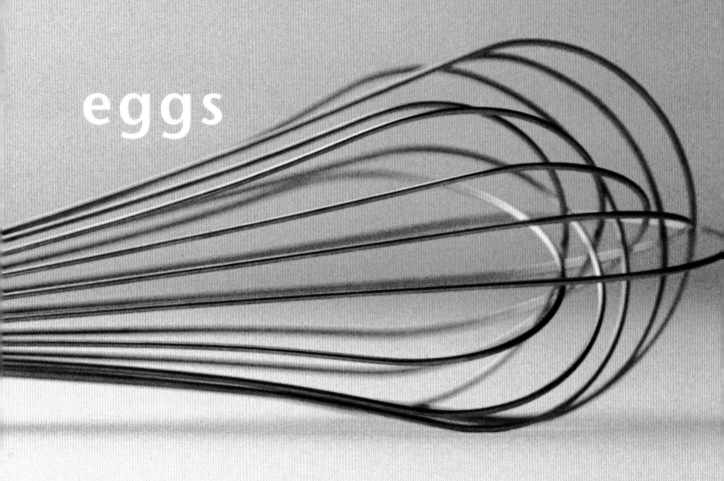

eggs

greek omelette with spinach, feta and dill

Most cooks will attribute their passion for food to childhood influences, especially those of their mother. I'm no different. My mother Robin was a passionate cook, always experimenting and producing innovative food, some of which I remember not wanting to eat! However, one thing she taught me to make very well was a great omelette. The secret to a fluffy omelette, she always said, was the addition of a little water. The other is not to cook it right through so that, when folded over, the center will be creamy. We usually ate omelettes as a light Sunday night supper, but they also make great breakfast food.

Heat ½ tablespoon of oil in a medium frypan. Add the onion, salt and pepper. Sauté over a medium heat for 4-5 minutes until the onion is tender, then add the garlic and cook for 1 minute. Transfer to a bowl and set aside.

Heat the remaining oil in the frypan and quickly wilt the spinach with ¼ teaspoon of salt over a high heat. Transfer to a colander, drain and cool. Squeeze out the excess moisture with your hands, then coarsely chop the spinach. Add the spinach to the onion, along with the lemon zest and dill. Season well with salt and pepper.

Season the egg with salt and pepper, add the water and whisk. Melt the butter in a seasoned omelette pan. When it is foaming, add half the egg mixture. With a spatula or fork, move the eggs toward the center of the pan as they begin to set on the edges. Tilt the pan so that the entire surface is covered again with wet eggs. As the eggs begin to set, place half the spinach mixture in the center, then sprinkle with half of the feta. Gently fold the omelette over and turn out onto a plate. Repeat with the second omelette.

MAKES 2 GENEROUSLY FILLED OMELETTES.

1 tablespoon olive oil

¼ medium red onion, thinly sliced

salt and pepper

1 clove garlic, finely chopped

1-2 bunches of spinach, stems removed and washed (about 8 cups)

zest of 1 lemon, grated

2 teaspoons fresh dill, chopped

6 eggs, beaten

¼ cup water

butter for pan

30 g (1 oz) feta cheese, crumbled

butter for pan

eggs foo yong with prawns

These delicious little egg pancakes can be served for brunch or as a light meal with the addition of some seedling greens or an Asian-style salad of julienned vegetables, sprouts and cilantro.

roughly chop the prawns. Beat the eggs with salt and pepper. Mix in the prawns, green onions and cilantro.

Heat a wok or frypan and add 2 teaspoons of oil and swirl to coat the center. Pour in 2 tablespoons of the egg mixture. When brown on the underside, turn and cook the other side. Transfer to a plate and keep warm. Repeat.

Wipe out the wok with a paper towel. Combine the soy sauce, sherry, vinegar, sugar and water in the wok or pan and stir over a medium heat until the sugar dissolves. Bring to a boil. Blend cornstarch and water, stir into the sauce and cook, stirring constantly, until thickened. Add the ginger and mix through.

Serve in a stack with the sauce and a sprinkling of cilantro leaves.

MAKES APPROXIMATELY 10.

250 g (9 oz) cooked prawns

6 eggs

salt and black pepper

6 green onions, finely chopped

1 tablespoon finely chopped cilantro leaves

peanut oil for frying

cilantro leaves to garnish

S A U C E

1 tablespoon light soy sauce

4 tablespoons dry sherry

2 tablespoons rice vinegar or white wine vinegar

2 tablespoons white sugar

$\frac{3}{4}$ cup water

1 tablespoon cornstarch blended with 2 tablespoons cold water

1 tablespoon shredded pickled ginger

basil frittata with asparagus

This dish is an all-time favorite of mine, adapted from a dish in Verdura *by Viana la Place, a cook who has inspired me a lot over the years. I only cook this particular dish when I can buy the very thin spears of asparagus early in the season. If you think there are a lot of asparagus recipes in this book, it's because it's one of my most loved foods.*

beat the eggs lightly. Add the basil, garlic and parmesan. Season to taste. If possible, let the mixture sit for 30 minutes to allow the flavors to infuse.

Trim the ends of the asparagus and cook in boiling water until just tender. Drain well and season with salt and a few drops of olive oil. Keep warm.

Heat the olive oil in a large sauté pan. Pour in a ladleful of the egg mixture and swirl, just as you would when making crèpes. Lower the heat a little and, when the frittata turns opaque, carefully flip it over. Repeat until you have made four thin frittatas.

Divide the asparagus into 4 portions and place each one on a frittata. Roll up, sprinkle with torn basil leaves and grated Parmesan.

SERVES 4.

6 eggs

*1 bunch basil, leaves only, chopped
  roughly, plus extra*

2 cloves garlic, finely chopped

¼ cup freshly grated Parmesan, plus extra

salt and freshly ground black pepper

500 g (1 lb) thin asparagus

*3 tablespoons extra virgin olive oil, plus
  extra*

herb frittata panino

When I asked some of the regular attendees at our 'Gourmet on the Run' classes what their favorite dishes were from the series, this one appeared every time. It's really snack food, perfect for a packed lunch or a picnic. How can something so simple be so delicious?

beat the eggs lightly in a bowl. Add the herbs, garlic and cheese and season to taste with salt and pepper. Mix well.

Preheat the grill.

Melt the butter in a small 20 cm (8") nonstick, ovenproof skillet over a high heat. When the butter foams and starts to brown, add the eggs. Reduce the heat and stir the eggs until curds form. Let the frittata cook until the bottom is firm but the top is still runny.

Place the pan under the grill and cook until the top is firm.

Lightly toast the bread and spread with butter. Fold the frittata in half and place between the slices.

Serve warm or at room temperature.

SERVES 1-2.

2 eggs

3 tablespoons mixed chopped herbs, e.g., basil, chives, marjoram

1 clove garlic, very finely chopped

1 tablespoon freshly grated Parmesan

salt and freshly ground black pepper

1 tablespoon unsalted butter

2-4 slices of country bread, depending on the size

picnic frittata

Italian-style frittatas are one of the quickest meals I know. If you have eggs in the house, then you can make a frittata. Sometimes I sauté slices of potato, sometimes I add chopped ham or sausage and sometimes I leave it plain with just fresh herbs for flavor. Served with a salad and some bread it makes a substantial meal. This one is as good warm as it is at room temperature.

Cook the pasta in plenty of boiling, salted water. Drain, toss with a little olive oil and cool.

Preheat the oven to 180°C/350°F.

Beat the eggs in a large bowl and add all the ingredients. Mix gently but well to combine.

Pour into a greased and lined 28 cm (11") pan and bake until the eggs are cooked and firm – about 40 minutes.

Allow to cool. Serve cut into wedges.

SERVES 6-8.

250 g (9 oz) pasta, any shape

12 eggs

12 slices pancetta (Italian bacon) or 6 slices bacon, grilled till crisp

4-6 sundried tomato halves, cut into slivers

1 cup grated zucchini

200 g (1½ cups) grated tasty cheese

50 g (½ cup) freshly grated Parmesan cheese

½ cup finely chopped red onion

½ cup parsley, chopped

salt and freshly ground black pepper to taste

1 tablespoon chile powder, or to taste (optional)

pasta

lasagne with
tomato cream sauce

Patricia Wells's books have always been a source of inspiration to me. This lasagne is adapted from her book Trattoria. *It's particularly simple to prepare.*

Preheat the oven to 175°C/350°F.

Cut the pasta to fit a baking dish approximately 23 x 36 cm (9 x 12"). In a large skillet, combine the oil, garlic, salt and chile, stirring to coat with oil. Cook over a moderate heat until the garlic turns golden but does not brown – 2 to 3 minutes. Add the tomatoes and simmer uncovered until the sauce begins to thicken – about 15 minutes. Add the cream, stir and heat for 1 minute. Taste and season with salt.

Bring a large pot of water to the boil. Cook the pasta sheets a few at a time in the salted boiling water. Float the cooked sheets in a large bowl of cold water with a spoonful of oil to prevent them sticking together. Remove and place the pasta on a clean, damp cloth. Continue until all the pasta is cooked.

Butter the baking dish and sprinkle with lemon zest.

Spoon about $\frac{1}{2}$ cup of the sauce over the bottom of the baking dish. Cover with pasta. Continue layering the lasagne and sauce, making sure that the final layer is pasta. Lay the thinly sliced mozzarella on top.

Place the baking dish in the center of the oven and bake until the cheese is melted and the dish is fragrant and bubbling – about 20 minutes. Remove from the oven and let sit for 10 minutes before cutting. Don't worry if the dish is a little runny when you serve it, that's the way it's meant to be.

SERVES 6-8.

1 quantity Basic Egg Pasta (see page 194), rolled as thinly as possible

1 tablespoon olive oil

zest of 1 lemon

250 g (8 oz) fresh whole milk mozzarella, thinly sliced

SAUCE

$\frac{1}{4}$ cup olive oil

4 garlic cloves, finely chopped

salt to taste

$\frac{1}{2}$ teaspoon crushed dried red chile

2 x 400 g (14 oz) tins peeled Italian plum tomatoes, crushed

1 cup cream

stuffed pasta with feta, tomatoes and mint

As soon as I saw this recipe in Joanne Weir's book From Tapas to Meze, *I just had to make it. The filling tastes just like Boursin cheese, something I developed a passion for when I lived in France in the '80s, so I sometimes make it just to spread on fresh bread. Traditionally this dish would be made with pasta. Wonton wrappers, however, really speed things up.*

to make the filling, place the feta, cream cheese and garlic in a food processor. Pulse to form a paste. With the motor running add the oil in a very slow and steady stream, allowing about 1 minute from start to finish. Add the chile, oregano, thyme, salt, pepper and lemon juice. Pulse several times. Set aside.

Place 1 tablespoon cheese filling in the center of each wonton wrapper, brush edges lightly with water and fold over to form a triangle. Seal the edges well and trim. Place on a heavily floured baking sheet.

Heat the olive oil in a skillet until hot. Add the tomatoes, reduce heat to medium and sauté uncovered for 2 minutes. Season well with salt and pepper.

Bring a large pot of salted water to the boil. Add the pasta and simmer 4-5 minutes or until done. Toss with the tomatoes, place on a serving dish and garnish with mint. Serve immediately.

MAKES 36.

FILLING

340 g (12 oz) feta cheese

170 g (6 oz) cream cheese

2 garlic cloves

1 tablespoon olive oil

1 small hot pickled chile, finely chopped

$\frac{1}{2}$ teaspoon dried oregano

$\frac{1}{4}$ teaspoon dried thyme

salt and freshly ground black pepper

1 tablespoon lemon juice

36 fresh wonton wrappers

SAUCE

$\frac{1}{4}$ cup extra virgin olive oil

2 cups seeded and chopped ripe tomatoes

salt and freshly ground black pepper

2 tablespoons fresh mint, chopped

spaghetti with
arugula, tomato and avocado

There are lots of easy uncooked sauces for pasta, where the warmth of the hot pasta brings out the flavors in the sauce beautifully. This one is very summery and could also include freshly blanched asparagus tips.

Slice the tomato halves very thinly. Place in a large bowl and add the arugula, avocado, garlic, olive oil, vinegar and chile flakes. Season with salt to taste. Toss gently, then let stand while you cook the pasta, stirring the salad gently from time to time.

Cook the pasta in a large pot of boiling, salted water until al dente. Drain pasta and transfer to the bowl containing the salad. Toss well and serve on warm dishes.

SERVES 4.

3-4 medium ripe tomatoes, peeled and seeded

large handful of baby arugula

1 ripe avocado, halved, pitted, peeled and thinly sliced crosswise

2 cloves garlic, finely chopped

5 tablespoons extra virgin olive oil

2 teaspoons white wine vinegar

$\frac{1}{8}$ teaspoon chile flakes or more to taste

sea salt

500 g (1 lb) dried spaghetti

pasta siciliana

The cuisine of Sicily is influenced by the intriguing mix of cultures that have played a part in the island's history. Some of these influences are apparent in this sauce – currants, rice vinegar and cayenne. This is another easy sauce that just needs a gentle warm through while the pasta is cooking.

In a large bowl combine the olives, cheese, currants, pinenuts and herbs. Mix well. Add the garlic, anchovy, shallot, lemon juice, vinegars and cayenne. Mix again and stir in the oil.

While the pasta is cooking, gently heat the sauce in a sauté pan until it is just warm; do not melt the Pecorino cheese. Drain the pasta and toss it with the sauce. Transfer to a serving bowl and garnish with plenty of Italian parsley.

SERVES 4-6.

$3/4$ *cup stuffed green olives, coarsely chopped*

$3/4$ *cup Kalamata olives, pitted and coarsely chopped*

$1/2$ *cup Pecorino cheese cut into small cubes*

$1/4$ *cup currants*

$1/2$ *cup pinenuts, toasted*

$1/4$ *cup fresh herbs, chopped (parsley, mint, basil, oregano etc.)*

2 cloves garlic, finely chopped

1 anchovy fillet, crushed to a paste

1 shallot, chopped

1 tablespoon lemon juice

1 tablespoon balsamic vinegar

1 tablespoon rice vinegar or white wine

$1/4$ *teaspoon cayenne pepper, or to taste*

1-1$1/2$ cups extra virgin olive oil

500 g (1 lb) spaghetti or linguine

Italian parsley to garnish

grilled vegetable lasagne

I have always avoided making lasagne for the simple fact that I end up with three pots and never enough sauce to finish the dish. However, when I watched Maggie Beer put this together during the week I spent in Italy, I was an instant convert. Why didn't I ever think to mix everything together this way?

I often liken the process of making fresh pasta by hand to breadmaking, deriving a similar level of satisfaction from each. Whenever I get my pasta machine out, I usually make several batches, leaving some as sheets and cutting the rest into linguine or fettuccine. It then goes straight from the freezer to the pot.

Cut the fresh pasta to fit an oblong or oval lasagne dish. Cook the sheets a few at a time in plenty of salted boiling water. Float the cooked sheets in a large bowl of cold water with a spoonful of oil to prevent them sticking together.

To make the béchamel sauce, heat the milk to scalding point and set aside. Melt the butter in another saucepan and stir in the flour. Cook, stirring, until you have a smooth golden paste. Gradually add the hot milk and stir until the sauce thickens and is very smooth. Cook gently for about 10 minutes. Season with salt, white pepper and nutmeg.

To make the parsley and cream sauce, wash and dry the parsley. Put the garlic in a saucepan and cover with cold water. Bring slowly to the boil, then pour off the water. Repeat this twice more. Slip the garlic out of its skin. Bring the garlic and cream slowly to simmering point, then remove the pan from the heat. The garlic will be quite soft. Add the parsley to the hot cream and immediately process in a blender to make a smooth green sauce. Taste for seasoning.

Preheat the oven to 180°C/350°F.

To assemble, drain the pasta and dry on a clean teatowel. Combine the vegetables with the two sauces, reserving about a cup of the béchamel sauce. Oil the lasagne dish and line it with a sheet of pasta. Cover with a layer of vegetables and top with another sheet of pasta. Continue until all the remaining pasta and vegetables have been used. Finish with a layer of the reserved béchamel sauce. Sprinkle with the Parmesan and drizzle with a little olive oil. Bake for about 30 minutes until bubbling and golden.

SERVES 6-8.

1 quantity basic egg pasta lasagne
   sheets (purchased or home-made)
olive oil
3-4 cups of sliced vegetables – zucchini,
   red onion, bell peppers, eggplant,
   field mushrooms (portabellos),
   brushed with olive oil and grilled
freshly grated Parmesan cheese

BÉCHAMEL SAUCE
600 ml (1 pint) milk
60 g (4 tablespoons) unsalted butter
60 g (12 tablespoons) plain flour
salt
freshly ground white pepper
freshly grated nutmeg

PARSLEY AND CREAM SAUCE
2 cups loosely packed flat-leaf parsley
   leaves
5 unpeeled cloves garlic
2 cups cream
salt
white pepper

linguine with grilled lemon chicken

Chicken thighs have much more flavor than the breast, so I use them frequently for barbecuing, always with the skin on during cooking to ensure succulent, flavorful meat. The sauce for this dish calls for the best extra virgin olive oil and the best pasta.

Combine the marinade ingredients. Toss the chicken well in the marinade, cover and refrigerate for up to two hours.

Preheat the grill or barbecue and grill the chicken until the skin is crisp and the chicken cooked through. Rest 5 minutes, then slice.

Meanwhile, bring a large pot of water to a boil.

Combine the sauce ingredients in a large bowl.

Cook the pasta in the boiling, salted water, drain and toss immediately, along with the chicken, in the sauce.

Shave over some Pecorino or Parmesan and serve.

Pass around a bowl of pesto separately.

SERVES 4.

6-8 boneless chicken thighs – skin on,
   trimmed of any excess fat
500 g (1 lb) linguine or spaghetti

MARINADE
$\frac{1}{2}$ cup good olive oil
juice of 2 juicy lemons
2 cloves garlic, crushed
a good grinding of black pepper

SAUCE
$\frac{1}{2}$ cup extra virgin olive oil
large handful of flat-leaf parsley leaves,
   chopped roughly
julienned zest of 2 lemons
salt and freshly ground black pepper
   to taste

GARNISH
fresh Pecorino or Parmesan cheese
basil pesto

penne with
abruzzi-style lamb sauce

This is a hearty winter dish to be eaten with plenty of crusty bread and a glass or two of a full-bodied red wine. Pecorino is a sheep's milk cheese from Italy. When mature it has a similar texture to Parmesan, which makes a good substitute if Pecorino is unavailable.

heat the oil in a large skillet and add the onion. Cook over a moderately high heat, stirring frequently, until the onion is pale gold. Add the bacon and rosemary and cook, stirring occasionally, until the fat is rendered. The bacon should remain soft.

Increase the heat. Add the lamb and cook until browned – about 5 minutes. Season with salt and pepper. Add the wine and simmer until evaporated – about 10 minutes.

Add the tomatoes and simmer gently until the fat begins to separate from the sauce – about 15 minutes.

Bring a large pot of water to a boil. Cook the penne in the boiling, salted water until al dente. Drain and transfer to a warmed bowl. Toss with the lamb sauce and cheese. Serve at once, passing around additional cheese at the table.

SERVES 4-6.

1 tablespoon extra virgin olive oil

$\frac{1}{4}$ cup chopped onion

2 slices bacon, finely chopped

1 tablespoon fresh rosemary, finely chopped

225 g (8 oz) boneless lamb, cut into very fine dice

salt and freshly ground black pepper

$\frac{1}{2}$ cup dry white wine

2 x 400 g (14 oz) cans Italian tomatoes, with juice, coarsely chopped

500 g (1 lb) penne pasta

$\frac{1}{3}$ cup Pecorino cheese, freshly grated

linguine with fresh tuna, puttanesca style

A few years ago most of the ingredients in this simple sauce would have been quite foreign to New Zealanders. Not any more. Now that most of them are staples in the pantry, this sauce is easy to throw together. Because it's quite hearty I prefer to use dried pasta.

bring a large pot of water to the boil.

Heat the oil in a frying pan over a moderate heat.

Add the garlic and chile and cook just until the garlic is fragrant.

Add the tomatoes and cook over a high heat until they start to break down. Add the capers and olives, reduce the heat and continue to cook until the sauce begins to thicken a little. Add the anchovies and tuna. Simmer until the tuna is barely cooked.

Cook the linguine in the boiling, salted water. Drain, then add to the sauce. Toss over a high heat to allow the pasta to absorb a little of the sauce. Place in a large bowl and serve immediately.

SERVES 4-6.

$\frac{1}{4}$ *cup extra virgin olive oil*

4-5 cloves garlic, finely chopped

$\frac{1}{2}$-*1 teaspoon chile powder or crushed dried chile*

400 g (14 oz) can Italian tomatoes, drained, seeded, chopped

1 tablespoon capers

$\frac{1}{4}$ *cup pitted black olives, cut into quarters*

3 anchovy fillets, soaked in milk, rinsed and chopped

500 g (1 lb) fresh tuna, cut into 2$\frac{1}{2}$ cm (1") dice

500 g (1 lb) dried linguine

risotto

The first class I ever taught at the Epicurean was in 1989, our first year. The theme was Italian food, and I cooked a saffron risotto. The response was extraordinary – we could tell, because not one person left without purchasing a bag of Arborio rice. What I had cooked was revolutionary – completely new. Well, to us anyway. It's taken a while, but risotto is now common on restaurant menus and the rice is readily available in supermarkets. However, each time I cook a risotto in class I get an underlying feeling that people still think it's difficult and time consuming. It's not! It is a very easy, one pot/one dish meal that you can have on the table in about 30 minutes. You just have to follow a few basic 'rules'. Once they are mastered, you can create your own versions using what's in season or in the fridge. I've experimented with different methods and strongly believe that the best results are gained by the traditional slow absorption method. You also need to use superfino Italian rice such as Arborio, Carnaroli or Vialone Nano. Other rices do not give the same creamy texture. I like US chef Todd English's description of how the finished risotto should be – 'When you spoon it out, risotto should sink on the plate, run a bit, and then stop.'

This is a dish that you should cook, not tucked away alone in the kitchen, but surrounded by friends who can share in the process and therefore really appreciate the end result.

orzo risotto with mussels and spicy sausage

I'm not sure whether this dish belongs with the pasta dishes or here with the risotti. Using orzo, a rice-shaped pasta from the Eastern Mediterranean, a very similar result to Italian risotto is achieved.

Cut the chorizo into 6 mm (½") cubes. Heat 1 tablespoon of olive oil in a large saucepan. Add the sausage and cook over a high heat until well browned. Remove from the pan, drain well on paper towels and discard all but 1 tablespoon of the fat. Add two-thirds of the garlic and cook until golden. Stir in the basil and oregano. Combine with the sausage and transfer to a small bowl.

Add the mussels to the saucepan and stir to coat with the oil remaining in the pan. Add the vermouth and bring to a boil over a high heat. Cover and cook until the mussels open – about 5-7 minutes. Remove them to a bowl as they open, covering to keep warm. Add the tomato and ¼ cup of the fish stock to the saucepan and boil over a high heat until the liquid is reduced by half. Stir in the sausage mixture.

Heat the remaining ¼ cup of olive oil in a heavy based pan. Add the onion and remaining garlic and cook over a moderate heat until soft and translucent. Add the orzo and stir until the pasta is well coated. Pour in the white wine and simmer, stirring occasionally, until absorbed.

Pour the remaining fish stock into a large measuring pitcher, add one-third to the orzo and cook over a moderate heat until absorbed. Stir in the sausage mixture and continue adding the stock and stirring until absorbed, as you would with a risotto. The orzo should be al dente and have a creamy consistency. Remove from the heat and stir in the butter and Parmesan cheese. Season with pepper.

Place the orzo risotto onto a warmed platter, arrange the mussels on top and serve.

SERVES 4.

250 g (9 oz) chorizo sausage

¼ cup plus 1 tablespoon olive oil

5 large cloves of garlic, finely chopped

a few leaves of fresh basil, finely chopped

1 sprig fresh oregano, finely chopped

500 g (1 lb) fresh baby mussels or cockles, cleaned and bearded

¼ cup dry vermouth

1 medium tomato, peeled, seeded and finely chopped

2½ cups fish stock (see page 196)

1 medium onion, finely chopped

1 cup orzo

½ cup dry white wine

3 tablespoons unsalted butter

½ cup freshly grated Parmesan cheese

freshly ground black pepper

asparagus risotto

I often celebrate the beginning of the asparagus season with this simple risotto. Contrary to the usual rule of barely cooking asparagus at all, the flavor of this risotto depends on adding the asparagus early in the cooking process and allowing it to break down. The result is a creamy, intensely flavored dish. However, save the tips to add just before serving. If you use a commercial stock, which is usually salted, dilute it well and taste before adding further salt.

Cook the asparagus in boiling, salted water until just tender. Drain, reserving 2 cups of the liquid, and cool. Cut the asparagus into small pieces and reserve the tips.

Bring the stock to a boil, then reduce to a simmer.

Melt half the butter in a large, heavy bottomed pot and sauté the onion until soft and transparent. Add the asparagus and, after 2 minutes, the rice. Stir until each grain is well coated with the butter.

Add a ladleful of the reserved cooking liquid. Stir until absorbed, then add some more. Continue in this way, adding a ladleful at a time. When you run out of cooking water, start adding the stock. After 20-25 minutes the rice will be very creamy and just firm in the middle. The degree of doneness is a very personal thing, so cook it until it is as you like it. Stir in the rest of the butter, the cheese, parsley and asparagus tips. Season with salt and pepper.

Transfer to a platter and serve at once with a leafy salad and some crusty bread.

SERVES 6.

500 g (1 lb) fresh asparagus, trimmed and rinsed

1-1½ liters (4-6 cups) chicken or vegetable stock (see page 196)

75 g (5 tablespoons) unsalted butter

2 large shallots or ½ small onion, finely chopped

500 g (1 lb) Arborio rice

50 g (½ cup) fresh Parmesan cheese, grated

1 tablespoon flat-leaf parsley, chopped

salt and freshly ground black pepper

shellfish risotto

What a wonderful way to showcase our green-lipped mussels, the best in the world! I like to pick small to medium-sized shells as I find them more tender and succulent than those that have been left to grow large.

Place the mussels in a pot with the white wine, cover and bring to a boil. Remove each mussel as it opens. Strain the cooking liquid through several layers of muslin and reserve. Remove the shells and discard. Set the mussels and reserved liquid aside.

Heat the oil in a large, heavy based pan. Sauté the onion and shallots over a low heat until soft. Add the fennel and sauté another 2-3 minutes. Add the rice and cook, stirring, 3 minutes longer, until each grain is coated with oil.

Bring the stock and reserved mussel liquid to a boil in another saucepan. Reduce the heat and keep at a simmer.

Add about 1 cup of hot liquid to the rice. Stir, and allow it to simmer. When the liquid has been absorbed, add $\frac{1}{2}$ cup, stir, and simmer. Continue adding the liquid, stirring constantly, until almost all the liquid has been added. Add the scallops, prawns and mussels. Continue cooking, adding liquid in $\frac{1}{4}$ cup amounts, until the seafood is cooked and the rice is creamy and just tender.

Stir in the black pepper and dill. Serve immediately. Parmesan would not normally be served with a seafood risotto.

SERVES 6.

1 kg (2 lb) fresh mussels

$\frac{1}{2}$ cup dry white wine

3 tablespoons olive oil

$\frac{1}{2}$ cup chopped onion

2 shallots, finely chopped

1 fennel bulb, cut into julienne

500 g (1 lb) Arborio rice

6 cups light fish stock (see page 196)

240 g (8 oz) scallops

240 g (8 oz) prawns, peeled and deveined

freshly ground black pepper

2 tablespoons fresh dill, chopped

risotto porcini casserole

Although not a true risotto, this dish makes a really hearty meal in colder weather. The porcini adds a richness to the flavour, but can be omitted if you can't lay your hands on any.

Place the porcini in a small bowl, cover with boiling water and let stand 30 minutes.

Melt half the butter in a large pan, add the green onion and carrot and sauté for 10 minutes. Add the rice and cook, stirring to coat with the butter for 1 minute.

Drain the porcini, slice them and strain the liquid through muslin to remove any grit. Pour this liquid over the rice. Add the wine and enough of the stock to completely cover the rice. Simmer, covered, over a low heat, adding more stock as needed, until the rice is tender – about 30 minutes.

Melt the remaining butter in a frying pan. Add the porcini and fresh mushrooms and sauté until tender. Stir in the garlic and parsley and simmer uncovered for 10 minutes. Season with salt and pepper.

Preheat the oven to 180°C/350°F. Spread half the rice in the bottom of a buttered baking dish and top with the mushroom mixture. Sprinkle generously with half the Parmesan and spread the remaining rice on top.

Whisk the cream, eggs and nutmeg together and pour evenly over the rice. Sprinkle the top with the remaining Parmesan. Bake until the top is puffed and brown – about 30 minutes.

SERVES 8.

15 g ($\frac{1}{2}$ oz) dried porcini mushrooms

120 g (4 oz) unsalted butter

4-5 green onions, finely chopped

2 carrots, peeled and finely chopped

2 cups Arborio rice

$\frac{1}{2}$ cup dry white wine

4-5 cups beef stock or brown chicken stock (see page 196)

500 g (1 lb) fresh mushrooms

3 cloves garlic, crushed

$\frac{3}{4}$ cup fresh flat-leaf parsley, chopped

salt and freshly ground black pepper

1-1$\frac{1}{2}$ cups Parmesan cheese, freshly grated

1 cup cream

2 eggs

pinch of ground nutmeg

pies & tarts

pissaladière

You could say this is just a pizza, except that it hails from the South of France, rather than Italy. Needless to say, you have to be a lover of anchovies – it's not nearly as good if you leave them out. Using a pizza stone ensures a crisp golden base.

Put the warm water in a large mixing bowl and sprinkle the dried yeast over the top. Leave until frothy. Add the oil to the water, then add the flour. Mix well to combine, tip out onto the counter and knead briefly until smooth. Leave to rise, covered, in a lightly oiled bowl until doubled in bulk (about 30 minutes).

Meanwhile, heat the olive oil in a frying pan and slowly cook the onion, garlic and thyme until golden. Stir in the tomatoes, increase the heat to high and cook until the liquid has evaporated and the mixture is thick – about 5 minutes. Discard the thyme.

Preheat a pizza stone or a metal baking sheet in a 250°C/500°F oven.

Roll out the dough to 6 mm (¼") on a lightly floured board and transfer to a well floured baking sheet or pizza peel.

Spread the tomato/onion mixture over the dough, arrange the anchovies in a spoke pattern and sprinkle the olives over the top.

Slide the pissaladière onto the hot stone or baking sheet and bake for 15-20 minutes until the base is crisp.

Garnish with sprigs of thyme and serve warm or at room temperature.

SERVES 6-8.

DOUGH

300 ml (10½ fl oz) lukewarm water

1 tablespoon active dried yeast

4 tablespoons olive oil

475 g (1lb) flour

TOPPING

2 tablespoons olive oil

5 medium onions, sliced thinly

2 large cloves garlic, sliced thinly

1 large sprig fresh thyme

2 large ripe tomatoes, peeled, cored, seeded and chopped

8 anchovy fillets in oil, drained

12 Kalamata olives

extra thyme for garnish

leek and goat cheese tart with mushrooms

A growing abundance of fresh goat cheeses being produced around the country adds considerable diversity to cooking with cheese. Di Lever's Saratoga cheeses are especially good when you want a mild goat flavor and a cheese that will soften without melting and brown nicely.

Place the flour, salt, thyme and butter in the food processor and process until the mixture resembles coarse breadcrumbs. Using the pulse button, add enough chilled water just to bind. Tip out onto a lightly floured board and bring together quickly and lightly with your hands. Form into a flat, round cake and roll out into a 34-36 cm (13½"-14½") round. Transfer to a baking sheet and chill.

Melt 2 tablespoons of the butter in a frypan over a medium heat. Add the leeks and sauté until translucent. Add the thyme, bayleaves and warm water. Cover and simmer until the leeks are nearly tender – about 15 minutes. Remove the lid and continue to cook until virtually all the liquid has evaporated – about 15 minutes. Remove the bayleaves and stir in the sour cream and goats cheese. Season well. The sauce should be thick and creamy.

Preheat the oven to 200°C/400°F.

In another frypan, melt the remaining butter. Add the mushrooms and sauté for a few minutes before adding the white wine and chicken stock. Cook until only a tablespoon of liquid remains, then remove from the heat.

Spread the leek mixture evenly over the pastry, leaving a 5 cm (2") border. Fold up the pastry to make a free-form tart. Bake until the pastry is crisp and golden – about 12-15 minutes. Add the mushrooms to the top and bake a further 5 minutes. Serve hot, cut in wedges and sprinkled with extra thyme.

SERVES 6.

PASTRY

1½ cups flour, chilled

¼ teaspoon salt

1 teaspoon fresh thyme leaves

130 g (4½ oz) unsalted butter, chilled

⅓-½ cup ice-cold water

FILLING

3 tablespoons unsalted butter

6 large leeks, white part only, washed well and finely sliced

1 tablespoon fresh thyme leaves, plus extra to garnish

2 fresh bayleaves

1 cup warm water

¼ cup sour cream

¼ cup crumbled fresh goat cheese

salt and freshly ground black pepper

100 g (4 oz) fresh button mushrooms, quartered

2 tablespoons white wine

¼ cup chicken stock (see page 196)

wild mushroom tart

It's only been in the last few years that we've been able to buy a wide selection of mushrooms. Here you can use just one type or several, depending on what's available. Tiny versions of these tarts make ideal cocktail bites. Don't underestimate ready-rolled pastry – it saves you hours!

Cut the woody ends off the mushrooms. Wipe with a damp cloth and, if large, slice into pieces.

Mash together the butter, garlic and parsley with a fork. Season with salt and pepper.

Preheat the oven to 250°C/500°F, or the highest setting.

Cut 15 cm (6") rounds of pastry and lay on a baking sheet. Alternatively, line 12 cm (5") tart pans with the pastry.

Divide the mushroom mixture into equal portions. Take a handful and press into a ball. Place in the center of each pastry round, leaving a 2½ cm (1") border. Crimp the pastry up to form a case. If using tart tins, just mound the mushrooms in the center.

Place about a tablespoon of the garlic butter on top of each tart. Bake, checking after 5 minutes and prick any bubbles with a skewer. Continue cooking for a further 10 minutes. The juices will run and give a delicious flavor to the pastry. Serve immediately, scattered with chives.

MAKES 5-6 TARTS.

450 g (1 lb) assorted fresh mushrooms – shiitake, oyster, brown, flats

125 g (4½ oz) unsalted butter

2 cloves garlic, crushed

handful of flat-leaf parsley, coarsely chopped

salt and freshly ground black pepper

1 packet ready-rolled puff pastry sheets, thawed

chopped chives to garnish

spinach and
blue cheese tarts

One of the most popular cookbooks to hit the shelves in recent years has been A Taste of Australia – The Bathers Pavilion Cookbook*, from the well-known restaurant on Sydney's Balmoral Beach. This tart is part Bathers Pavilion (the filling) and part Julie le Clerc (the pastry). Julie is a regular face at Epicurean, where she shares many secrets from her fabulous Garnet Road Food Store.*

Place the flour, salt and paprika in a food processor and pulse briefly to sift. With the motor running, drop in the butter and process to fine crumbs. Add the sour cream and process just enough to incorporate. Tip out onto the counter and bring together quickly into a ball. Wrap and chill for 10 minutes. Roll out to 3 mm ($\frac{1}{8}$") thickness, cut and fit the pastry into 8 x 12 cm (5") tart pans with removable bases. Lightly prick the pastry with a fork. Place the tarts in the refrigerator to rest for 30 minutes.

Melt a little butter in a pan and quickly fry off the spinach until dry. Set aside.

Heat the olive oil in a medium frypan over a low heat. Add the onion and cook very slowly until deep golden brown in color and very soft. This will take about 30 minutes. Place the cooked onions in a sieve and drain off any remaining oil. Set aside.

Preheat the oven to 200°C/400°F.

Place baking paper and baking beans into the tart shells to bake blind (see page 192). Bake for about 8 minutes until the pastry is cooked and just starting to brown.

In a bowl, mix together the egg yolks and mascarpone until well blended. Stir through the blue cheese.

Place a little of the onion in the bottom of each tart shell, a few walnut pieces, then a little of the spinach. Grind over a little black pepper and top with the cheese mixture.

Bake the tarts for 10-12 minutes until puffed and golden, but still creamy in the middle.

MAKES 8 TARTS.

PASTRY

1$\frac{3}{4}$ cups flour

$\frac{1}{2}$ teaspoon salt

1 teaspoon paprika

125 g (4$\frac{1}{2}$ oz) unsalted butter, diced

$\frac{1}{3}$ cup sour cream

FILLING

butter

$\frac{3}{4}$ cup frozen spinach, thawed and squeezed dry

200 ml (7 fl oz) olive oil

4 onions, finely sliced

2 egg yolks

120 g ($\frac{1}{2}$ cup) mascarpone

300 g (11 oz) strong flavored blue cheese, crumbled

freshly ground black pepper

2 tablespoons walnuts, chopped (optional)

ratatouille tart

Make good use of late summer vegetables in this tart. Baking the pastry blind results in a crisp light base and allows the tart to be made ahead. Serve it warm or at room temperature with a salad on the side.

Preheat the oven to 200°C/400°F.

Roll out the pastry and line a 20 cm (8") tart pan with a removable base. Chill in the refrigerator for 15 minutes. Bake blind (see page 192) and brush lightly with olive oil when it is removed from the oven.

Brush a baking sheet with olive oil. Place the onion and whole cloves of garlic on the tray and toss in a little olive oil. Roast for about 15 minutes, turning once, until the vegetables are golden and caramelized.

In a large frypan, heat 1 teaspoon of olive oil over a medium heat. Add the eggplant and sauté for a few minutes. Add the crushed garlic, sauté one minute and add the fresh and sundried tomatoes, the thyme and salt and pepper to taste. Simmer for 10 minutes, then stir in the balsamic vinegar.

Arrange the onion slices in the base of the tart pan and top with the eggplant mixture. Sprinkle over half the Parmesan, then place the tomato slices and whole garlic on top. Drizzle over the remaining olive oil and scatter the rest of the Parmesan. Bake for 25 minutes until bubbly and golden.

SERVES 4.

1 batch rich shortcrust pastry (see page 195)

2 teaspoons olive oil

2 medium onions, sliced

4 cloves garlic, whole, peeled

2 cloves garlic, crushed

250 g (9 oz) eggplant, diced

250 g (9 oz) ripe tomatoes, diced

1 sundried tomato, drained and sliced

1 tablespoon chopped fresh thyme

salt and freshly ground black pepper

1 tablespoon balsamic vinegar

55 g (2 oz) Parmesan cheese, sliced into shards with a vegetable peeler

4 large slices of tomato

pumpkin and
blue cheese galette

Pumpkin and blue cheese are made to go together. This freeform tart uses an easy yeasted dough, but you could use puff pastry.

Preheat the oven to 190°C/375°F. Cut the pumpkin in half and scrape out the seeds and fibers. Lightly brush each side of the pumpkin with olive oil, then season with salt and pepper. Place the garlic cloves in the cavities and turn the pumpkin halves cut-side down on a baking sheet. Bake for about 1 hour until the flesh is tender.

In a bowl stir together the water, yeast and sugar. Let stand in a warm place until bubbly – about 10 minutes.

In another bowl, toss the flour with the salt and make a well. Add the egg, butter and yeast mixture. Using a wooden spoon, blend the flour into the liquid ingredients to form a soft dough. Turn out onto a floured board and knead until smooth. Place the dough in a lightly greased bowl, cover with plastic wrap and let rise until doubled in bulk (about 45 minutes). Punch down the dough and allow to rest briefly before rolling out.

Scoop out the pumpkin into a large bowl and mash with a fork until fairly smooth. Squeeze the garlic out of its skin and mash. In a small skillet, warm 2 teaspoons of olive oil over a low heat. Add the onion and sage and cook until the onion is soft and beginning to brown. Add to the pumpkin mixture along with the garlic and Parmesan. Mix well, season and stir in half the blue cheese.

Preheat the oven to 200°C/400°F. On a lightly floured baking tray, roll out the dough into a 36 cm (14") round. Spread the vegetable mixture onto the dough, leaving a 5 cm (2") border. Sprinkle the remaining blue cheese on top. Fold over the edges of the dough and brush with beaten egg.

Bake the galette until the crust is nicely browned – about 25 minutes.

SERVES 6-8.

1 kg (2 lb) butternut pumpkin

olive oil

salt and freshly ground black pepper

1 small head of garlic, broken up but
 not peeled

1 small onion, finely chopped

10 fresh sage leaves, chopped
 (1½ teaspoons dried)

½ cup freshly grated Parmesan cheese

⅔ cup crumbled blue cheese

1 large egg, beaten

YEAST DOUGH

⅓ cup lukewarm water

1 teaspoon active dried yeast

½ teaspoon sugar

1½ cups flour

½ teaspoon salt

1 large egg, beaten

3 tablespoons unsalted butter, softened

tarte tatin provençal

It's unfortunate that I can't remember where I first came across this recipe because it is now in my repertoire of favorites. The red onions in this savory version of the famous apple tarte tatin become gloriously sweet through slow cooking. If you are unnerved by the upside down aspect of this tart, I can assure you it always turns out of the pan perfectly – as long as you do it while still warm.

Place the flour, butter and salt in the food processor. Blend until the mixture resembles coarse breadcrumbs. Using the pulse button, slowly add enough ice water (about 2-3 tablespoons) to form a dough. Press into a flat disc shape, wrap in plastic wrap and refrigerate for at least 30 minutes.

Melt the butter in a heavy 25 cm (10") ovenproof frying pan. Sprinkle with sugar and remove from the heat. Cut 4 onions in half sideways and arrange cut-side down over the base of the pan. Slice the remaining onions and scatter over and around the onion halves. Sprinkle with thyme and season to taste. Cook, shaking the pan occasionally, over a low to medium heat for 15 minutes, or until the onion halves are golden on the base. Pour over the stock and vinegar, bring to the boil, reduce heat and simmer, covered, for 25-30 minutes, or until the onions are tender. Remove the lid, increase the heat and cook for about 5 minutes, or until the liquid has reduced to a thick syrup. Remove from the heat and allow to cool for 20 minutes.

Preheat the oven to 190°C/375°F.

Arrange the pepper, tomatoes, black olives and anchovies among the onion halves.

Roll out the pastry on a lightly floured surface to a disc slightly larger than the frying pan. Place the pastry over the ingredients and tuck in the edges to fit snugly around the onions.

Bake for 25-30 minutes or until the pastry is cooked and golden. Let rest for 5 minutes before inverting onto a serving plate.

Serve warm or at room temperature, garnished with thyme sprigs.

SERVES 6.

PASTRY

185 g (1¼ cups) plain flour

100 g (½ cup) chilled unsalted butter, chopped

½ teaspoon salt

ice-cold water

FILLING

20 g (¾ oz) unsalted butter

2 teaspoons sugar

6 medium red onions

1 teaspoon fresh thyme leaves

salt and freshly ground black pepper

250 ml (1 cup) chicken stock (see page 196)

1-2 teaspoons balsamic vinegar

1 red bell pepper, roasted, peeled and sliced (see page 195)

3 sundried tomatoes, sliced

12 Kalamata olives

optional – rolled anchovies

fresh thyme to garnish

one dish meals

couscous and vegetable stew

Couscous is another grain that can be quickly and easily prepared. A festive and traditional Moroccan or North African dish, it differs from rice or polenta by being man-made. The tiny pellets are produced by rubbing a paste of semolina through a sieve, after which they are dried. Today's instant variety takes only a few minutes to cook and can be used in salads, pilafs and soups. Turn this dish into a soup by adding only half the couscous and increasing the chicken stock to 2 liters.

Heat the olive oil in a large saucepan. Add the onion and cook over a low heat until soft, then add the chicken and cook a further 3 minutes. Add the spices and tomato paste and stir over a low heat for a few minutes until fragrant. Add the tomatoes, stock and all the vegetables, bring to a simmer, cover and cook over a low heat for 15 minutes or until the vegetables are just tender. Gradually pour in the couscous and cook, stirring occasionally, for 5 minutes.

Remove the cinnamon sticks and serve in deep bowls sprinkled with cilantro.

SERVES 6.

2 tablespoons olive oil

1 onion, chopped

2 chicken breasts, cut into bite-size pieces

2 cinnamon sticks

$\frac{1}{2}$ teaspoon ground cardamom

$\frac{1}{2}$ teaspoon paprika

$\frac{1}{4}$ teaspoon chile powder

1 tablespoon tomato paste

400 g (14 oz) can of tomatoes, drained and chopped

$1\frac{1}{2}$ liters (6 cups) chicken stock (see page 196)

1 zucchini, chopped

1 carrot, peeled and chopped

4 pattipan squash, quartered

1 cup instant couscous

2 tablespoons cilantro, chopped

roasted asparagus with olive oil and parmesan

Asparagus prepared this way can be eaten for breakfast, brunch or lunch. A whole platter also looks very festive on a buffet. Because of their unique flavors, use pancetta (Italian bacon) or prosciutto (Parma ham) if you can find them.

Preheat the oven to 225°C/450°F. Toss the asparagus with 1 tablespoon of the olive oil and season lightly with salt and pepper.

Place in a small ovenproof dish and roast for approximately 4-6 minutes until just cooked. Alternatively, grill on the barbecue. Test with the point of a knife – there should be only a fraction of resistance.

While the asparagus is roasting, grill or fry the pancetta until it starts to render its fat and become crisp. Chop coarsely.

Transfer the asparagus to a serving plate and drizzle with the rest of the olive oil. Squeeze over lemon juice, scatter over the pancetta and egg. Lastly, shave shards of Parmesan over the top and serve immediately.

SERVES 1.

FOR EACH PERSON

8 asparagus spears

3 tablespoons olive oil

salt and freshly ground black pepper

6 thin slices pancetta, prosciutto or bacon

juice of $\frac{1}{2}$ lemon

1 egg, hardboiled and chopped

fresh Parmesan cheese

warm prawn and scallop salad with arugula

Warm salads are one of the by-products of nouvelle cuisine that seem to have survived. The combination of crisp salad and warm meat or fish is delicious when eaten immediately. This dish makes a good summer lunch or a first course.

arrange the selected salad greens, asparagus and snow peas on a platter.

Combine the cilantro, five-spice powder, chile and garlic. Add the prawns and scallops and toss to coat lightly. Heat $2\frac{1}{2}$ tablespoons of sesame oil in a wok until hot. Add the seafood mixture and green onion and toss over high heat for 1-3 minutes or until opaque. Remove and immediately place on top of the salad greens.

Add the remaining oil, lemon juice and soy sauce to the wok and heat through. Drizzle this 'dressing' over the salad and sprinkle with pinenuts, sesame seeds and cilantro.

SERVES 3-4 AS A LUNCH DISH, 5 AS A FIRST COURSE.

arugula and/or mixed salad greens

asparagus, cooked and refreshed

75 g ($2\frac{1}{2}$ oz) snow peas, strings removed, then blanched and refreshed

2 tablespoons cilantro, chopped

1 teaspoon five-spice powder

1 fresh red chile, seeded and finely sliced

1 clove garlic, crushed

15 medium-sized green prawns, peeled and deveined, with tails left intact

15 scallops with roe, cleaned

$\frac{1}{4}$ cup sesame oil

4 green onions, sliced

2 teaspoons lemon juice

1 tablespoon soy sauce

2 tablespoons pinenuts, toasted

2 teaspoons sesame seeds, toasted

extra cilantro for garnish

cabbage stuffed with bacon
and lentils with mustard sauce

Hearty winter fare! And what a great way to use cabbage. Steaming ensures that it stays green and still has a bit of bite to it. The steamer with the largest surface area is a bamboo one. Sit it over a pot or, better still, inside a wok. These steamers usually have two layers, making it possible to cook all the packets at once.

Cut the bacon into strips and cook in a hot pan until it starts to crisp. Remove, drain on paper towels and place into a bowl. Add the oil to the pan, add the red cabbage and stir in the juniper berries. Cook until the cabbage is bright and shiny and has softened a little, but still retains its crunch. Remove and add to the bacon.

Chop the apples, add to the pan with the hazelnuts and raisins. Cook over a gentle heat until the apples color a little. Splash in the vinegar, then stir in the redcurrant jelly. Allow to bubble, then add the bacon and cabbage. Stir in the cooked lentils. Season with salt and pepper.

Spread out the cabbage leaves and divide the stuffing between them. Fold up the leaves to make a small packet. Secure with string and pack into a steamer. Steam, covered, for about 8 minutes or until thoroughly hot.

To make the mustard sauce, pour the cream into a shallow pan. Stir in the mustard and season with salt and pepper. Taste for seasoning, adding more mustard if you wish. Allow the sauce to bubble for 2-3 minutes until it has thickened slightly.

SERVES 4.

8 large green cabbage leaves, blanched
   and cooled

200 g (7 oz) smoked bacon

2 tablespoons vegetable oil

200 g (7 oz) red cabbage, shredded

$1\frac{1}{2}$-2 teaspoons juniper berries, lightly
   crushed

2 apples

$\frac{1}{4}$ cup hazelnuts, toasted

$\frac{1}{4}$ cup raisins

4 tablespoons wine or cider vinegar

2 tablespoons redcurrant jelly

120 g ($\frac{3}{4}$ cup) brown or green lentils,
   cooked

salt and freshly ground black pepper

FOR THE SAUCE

250 ml (1 cup) cream

6 tablespoons Dijon mustard

salt and pepper

polenta with
grilled summer vegetables

This is a dish with dozens of possible variations. The polenta can remain the same, just alter the combinations on top depending on what's available. That might include asparagus or fennel bulb, root vegetables during the winter months, and so on, plus feta cheese, olives, capers or anchovies.

bring the stock to a boil. Slowly pour the polenta into the boiling stock, whisking constantly. Continue stirring with a wooden spoon for 5-10 minutes.

Stir in the butter and Parmesan, season well and tip out onto a greased tray. Spread out to approximately 5 mm (2″) thick.

Allow to cool, then cut into wedges.

Preheat the grill of the barbecue or oven.

Brush all the vegetables except the tomatoes with olive oil and grill or barbecue until tender and well coloured.

Brush the polenta with olive oil and grill both sides until golden.

Place on a platter and top with the grilled vegetables and tomatoes. Tuck a few basil leaves in amongst the vegetables. Drizzle with good olive oil, season well with salt and pepper and sprinkle with shavings of Parmesan.

SERVES 6.

FOR THE POLENTA

1½ liters light chicken stock

300 g (2 cups) instant polenta

60 g (3 tablespoons) butter

4 tablespoons freshly grated Parmesan cheese

sea salt and freshly ground black pepper

FOR THE VEGETABLES

extra virgin olive oil

1 large eggplant, sliced thickly

2 red bell peppers, halved, seeded and sliced

2 zucchini, sliced thickly on the diagonal

2 ripe beefsteak tomatoes, sliced

a few basil leaves

salt and freshly ground black pepper

freshly grated or shaved Parmesan cheese for garnish

south indian spicy lentil stew

Everyone who has tasted this dish has been surprised how good it is. It has that comfort factor and is therefore an ideal dish to serve on a cold winter's evening, either on its own with the Cilantro, Ginger and Chile Dosa on page 39 or as part of an Indian feast that contains rice and other dishes. In India it would be served year round. You'll find all the ingredients, including the sambhar masala (a mixture of dahl, chile and spices), at most Indian stores. The inspiration for this dish came from Flatbreads and Flavors *by Naomi Duguid and Jeffrey Alford, Canadian photographers with a passion for food.*

In a large saucepan bring the water to a boil. Add the dahl, tomatoes, okra, carrots, potatoes, turmeric, salt and tamarind paste or lemon juice. Stir and bring back to a boil. Reduce the heat slightly and cook until the dahl is tender – approximately 30 minutes; add more water if necessary.

Meanwhile, in a heavy skillet, heat the oil and lightly fry the ground cilantro and cumin over a medium heat. Add the mustard seeds, chile and curry leaves and fry for 2 minutes, covering the skillet as the seeds pop. Add the fried spices to the cooked dahl and vegetables. Add the sambhar masala and mix well.

Serve with fresh Cilantro, Ginger and Chile Dosa (see page 39).

The stew can be prepared up to 2 hours in advance.

SERVES 6 WITH DOSA.

4 cups water

1 cup masur dahl (red lentils) or mung dahl (yellow lentils)

2 tomatoes, cut into large chunks

5-6 large okra, halved lengthways

2 carrots, cut into large chunks

2 potatoes, cut into large chunks

1 tablespoon turmeric

2 teaspoons salt

2 teaspoons tamarind paste or 1 tablespoon lemon juice

1 tablespoon vegetable oil

1 tablespoon cilantro seeds, ground

1 teaspoon cumin seeds, ground

1 tablespoon black mustard seeds

1-2 jalapeño peppers, seeded and chopped

6-8 dried curry leaves

1 tablespoon sambhar masala

*South Indian Spicy Lentil Stew (top),
Cilantro, Ginger and Chile Dosa
(bottom)*

fish & seafood

New Zealand is blessed with clean waters and an abundance of seafood. Wonderful markets offer an ever changing selection, so when you are choosing fish look for firm, glossy fillets with a translucent appearance or whole fish with bright shiny eyes, clear unbroken skin and bright red gills. It should slip through your hands like a cake of wet soap. Any fish should have a 'clean' smell, slightly fishy – never the odor of ammonia.

Store fish, fillets or whole, under several thicknesses of wet paper towels in the refrigerator.

fillet of john dory with pinenuts, onions and yellow raisins

Normally it is sacrilege not to serve fish as soon as it is cooked. This dish, however, benefits from being left to marinate in its sweet/sour dressing for a few hours before being served at room temperature.

dredge the pieces of fish in flour. Heat 4-5 tablespoons of oil in a large, heavy skillet over a medium-high heat. Sauté the fillets quickly in batches until golden brown, adding more oil as needed. Transfer to a large, shallow serving dish and sprinkle with pepper.

Heat an additional 3 tablespoons of oil in the same skillet and sauté the onion for 8-10 minutes until golden but not browned. Scatter over the fish, along with the yellow raisins and pinenuts.

To make the dressing, combine the wine, vinegar and honey. Pour over the fish. Let cool to room temperature. Cover and refrigerate for 3-4 hours or overnight. Bring back to room temperature before serving.

SERVES 6.

650 g (1 lb 4 oz) fillet of John Dory, cut on the diagonal into $2\frac{1}{2}$ cm (1") strips

flour

$\frac{1}{2}$-$\frac{3}{4}$ cup extra virgin olive oil

freshly ground black pepper to taste

2 medium onions, cut into slivers

6 tablespoons yellow raisins, soaked in hot water for 10 minutes and drained

$\frac{3}{4}$ cup pinenuts, toasted

$1\frac{1}{2}$ cups dry white wine

6 tablespoons white wine vinegar

5-6 tablespoons honey

tunisian fish tagine

Alister Little, an English chef, has published several books that have been hugely popular in New Zealand. This recipe is adapted from one in his book Food of the Sun. *Kaffir lime leaves can be purchased dried or plant your own tree. They can be container grown and probably won't fruit, but it's the leaves that are used most frequently for their unique fragrance. The use of them in this dish is probably not traditional – a little bit of 'fusion' – so don't worry if you can't find any, just use the zest of lime or lemon instead.*

toast the cumin seeds in a dry pan for 2-3 minutes over a low heat. Grind to a powder in a mortar and pestle or in a spice grinder and set aside.

Seed the chiles and cut into julienne strips.

Place half of the olive oil in one large frypan and half in a nonstick pan with a lid. Put the potato into the nonstick pan. Add the turmeric and fry, tossing and turning the potatoes.

At the same time in the other pan, fry the onion and celery, stirring occasionally. When the onion begins to soften, add the garlic, lime leaves, chiles, cumin, paprika and saffron. Cook for a further 2-3 minutes, then season lightly with salt and pepper and turn off the heat. Leave in the pan while the potatoes finish cooking.

As soon as the potatoes are cooked, season the fish steaks with salt and pepper and put them on top of the potatoes. Spoon the onion mixture over and around the steaks and pour over the tomatoes. Bring to the boil over a medium-high heat, immediately lower it and cover. Cook gently for 7-10 minutes or until the fish is just cooked. Taste and season.

Serve in large warmed bowls, sprinkled with cilantro.

SERVES 4.

4 teaspoons cumin seeds

2 fresh red chiles

5 tablespoons olive oil

700 g (1 lb 6 oz) potatoes, peeled and cut into 1cm (½") cubes

1½ teaspoons turmeric

2 medium onions, sliced into thin rings

1 stalk of celery, finely chopped

2 garlic cloves, chopped

4 Kaffir lime leaves, optional

2 teaspoons paprika

a pinch of saffron threads infused in 1½ tablespoons warm water

4 x 150-170 g (5-6 oz) fish steaks, cod or hapuku

salt and pepper

2 x 400 g (14 oz) cans Italian tomatoes, puréed and sieved (about 2 cups)

large handful of cilantro to garnish

baby snapper on
thai curry vegetables

From time to time I enjoy cooking whole fish. It brings back childhood memories of the flounder we often ate, done quickly in the pan and served with nothing but a squeeze of lemon and a grind of pepper. Baby snapper are exceptionally sweet but, if they aren't around, use fillets with the skin on.

to make the sauce, heat the oil in a heavy saucepan and sweat the onion, cilantro, garlic and cumin, covered, over a low heat for 5 minutes. Stir in the curry paste, cover and cook over a low heat, stirring occasionally, for 5 minutes longer. Stir in the coconut milk and lemon juice and simmer for 20 minutes uncovered. Remove from the heat and stand for 10 minutes. Skim the surface to remove any excess oil.

Preheat the oven to 180°C/350°F.

Heat a little oil in a frying pan (or use the barbecue) and sear the fish over a high heat for 1½ minutes on each side or until golden. Transfer to an oven dish and bake for 6-8 minutes or until the fish flakes when tested with a fork.

Meanwhile, heat 1 tablespoon of oil in a frying pan or wok and cook the vegetables, garlic and cilantro leaves over a medium heat for 3 minutes or until the vegetables are cooked but still crisp. Add half the sauce and bring to the boil.

Arrange the vegetables on a serving platter and spoon on a generous amount of sauce. Place the fish on top and garnish with chopped chives.

SERVES 4.

olive oil

4 whole baby snapper, cleaned and scaled, sides scored with knife 3-4 times

4 cups mixed julienned vegetables, including bell pepper, carrot, red onions, zucchini and chives

1 clove garlic, crushed

½ bunch of cilantro, chopped

1 bunch of chives, chopped to garnish

SAUCE

1 tablespoon olive oil

2 red onions, diced

1 bunch of cilantro, finely chopped

3 cloves garlic, finely chopped

1 teaspoon ground cumin

2 tablespoons red curry paste

2¾ cups coconut milk

juice of 2 lemons

mussels saganaki

I have no idea of the origins of this dish. It could be Mediterranean although the mint suggests Turkey. Whatever, it is one of the most delicious ways to eat mussels. Serve them in a shallow bowl with steamed rice.

Clean and beard the mussels. Put the mussels and water in a deep wide pan and cook until they open – about 3-5 minutes. Transfer them to a bowl, in order to catch their juices. Strain and reserve the cooking liquid. When they are cool enough to handle, remove from their shells and sprinkle with black pepper and lemon juice. Add any juice to the saved cooking liquid.

In a frypan, heat the oil over a medium heat. Add 2 teaspoons of the chile and parsley and cook 1 minute, stirring. Add the cooking liquid, mint, oregano, garlic, hot chile flakes, mustard, tomatoes and a good grind of black pepper and quickly bring to a boil. Cook over a medium heat for 5 minutes, stirring often, or until the sauce has thickened to about $1\frac{1}{4}$ cups. If desired, add the remaining green chile to taste. Add the mussels and warm gently. Allow to cool slightly before adding the cubes of feta. Stir and cook for a few minutes. Do not allow the sauce to boil.

Season to taste and serve with a sprinkling of parsley.

SERVES 4-6.

$1\frac{1}{2}$ *kg ($3\frac{1}{2}$ lb) fresh mussels*

$\frac{1}{2}$ *cup water*

freshly ground black pepper

lemon juice

1 tablespoon olive oil

1 long green chile, seeded and finely chopped

$\frac{1}{3}$ *cup flat-leaf parsley, chopped*

5 large mint leaves, shredded

$\frac{1}{2}$ *teaspoon dried oregano*

1 small clove garlic, crushed

pinch of hot chile flakes

1 teaspoon powdered mustard

$\frac{1}{2}$ *cup peeled, seeded and chopped tomatoes, fresh or canned*

100 g (4 oz) feta cheese, cut into cubes

sea salt

flat-leaf parsley for garnish

grilled whole fish
with herb paste

Pastes like this one can be used under the skin of chicken breasts or patted onto the back of lamb racks. Vary it with different herbs, or the addition of ground nuts, spices or lemon zest. They can turn simple grilled meats into something spectacular.

Place the garlic and all the herbs in a food processor, and pulse to chop roughly. Add the salt and pepper and continue to process until the herbs begin to form a paste. Drizzle in some olive oil and work the oil into the herbs to form a smooth mixture.

Make 4 shallow slashes on each side of the fish. With your fingers, work the herb paste into the slashes, rubbing some into the cavity as well. Lay the fish on a platter to marinate for about 30 minutes.

Heat a barbecue grill or ridged stovetop griddle until very hot. Carefully lay the fish onto the grill. Cook the fish until a thin crust forms on the skin, which enables you to turn it with a spatula. As the fish cooks, baste it with a little oil. Allow approximately 2-4 minutes per side. Garnish with lemon wedges.

SERVES 4.

1 garlic clove

good handful of fresh basil leaves

1 sprig fresh rosemary, leaves only, very finely chopped

$\frac{1}{4}$ cup coarsely chopped flat-leaf parsley

1-2 teaspoons sea salt or to taste

freshly ground black pepper to taste

extra virgin olive oil

4 small whole fish such as snapper, approx. 500 g (1 lb) each, cleaned and scaled

lemon wedges

chermoula fish with chickpea pasta

This one is for cilantro aficionados. Combined with the spices it gives a fresh, fragrant flavour to the fish. Chermoula is a favorite marinade not only for firm-fleshed fish but also for chicken or lamb. The salad is a particularly good partner but could happily stand on its own.

Place all chermoula ingredients into a food processor and blend.

Pour over the fish and allow to marinate for at least an hour.

Cook chickpeas in fresh simmering water for 1 hour or until tender.

Cook pasta in plenty of boiling salted water until al dente.

Add the olive oil and thyme to a large pan and heat gently to infuse oil. Add the vegetables and cook until soft. Add the chickpeas, pasta, salt, pepper and herbs and heat through. Transfer to a platter.

Preheat the barbecue, stovetop grill or the grill in the oven.

Grill fish, drizzle with remaining marinade and place on top of the chickpea pasta salad.

SERVES 6.

6 fish steaks (salmon, hapuku, etc.)

CHERMOULA MARINADE
handful fresh cilantro
handful of flat-leaf parsley
2 cloves garlic, smashed
1 teaspoon each ground cumin,
  cilantro, paprika
juice of 2 lemons
grated zest of 1 lemon
2 tablespoons olive oil

SALAD
1 cup dried chickpeas, soaked overnight
  (or 2 cups canned chickpeas)
1 cup small dried pasta
1 tablespoon olive oil
3 sprigs of fresh thyme
1 red bell pepper, seeded and diced
3 zucchini, diced
3 ripe tomatoes, diced
salt and freshly ground black pepper
1 tablespoon basil leaves
1 tablespoon flat-leaf parsley, chopped

grilled niçoise salad

This is a spectacular barbecue dish where everything gets grilled at the same time and assembled together on one platter. The dressing makes a rather good dipping sauce for raw vegetables, too. Remember that tuna should still be very rare in the middle – cook it through and it will be dry and unpalatable.

In a food processor, blend the anchovies, garlic, mustard and lemon juice until combined. With the machine running, slowly add the olive oil, a few drops at first, and then in a slow, steady stream. Season with salt and pepper.

Heat a barbecue or a stovetop grill. Lightly coat the potatoes, onion, tomatoes and beans with oil and sprinkle with salt. Lightly brush the tuna with oil and sprinkle with salt and a little freshly ground black pepper. Put the potatoes over a medium-low heat and cook until they are fork tender and roasted looking, turning occasionally to keep them from sticking – 30 to 35 minutes in total. Put the onion, tomatoes and green beans on a medium-high part of the grill. Grill the vegetables until they are lightly charred and tender, moving the ingredients around so they don't overcook. As the vegetables come off the grill, transfer them to a tray and drizzle with the dressing, toss lightly and cover with foil to keep warm.

Meanwhile, grill the tuna over a medium-high heat until it is still pink in the middle. Let cool for a few minutes and slice.

Place the salad leaves on a platter and arrange the vegetables and tuna on top. Garnish with the capers, eggs, anchovies and olives. Drizzle with a little more dressing and sprinkle with shredded basil and serve.

SERVES 6.

DRESSING – MAKES 1 CUP

4 anchovies, finely chopped

1 clove garlic, chopped

2 tablespoons Dijon mustard

4 teaspoons fresh lemon juice

$\frac{1}{2}$ cup extra virgin olive oil

salt and freshly ground black pepper

SALAD

8-10 small red skinned potatoes

1 large red onion, sliced 1 cm ($\frac{1}{2}$") thick

2 medium tomatoes, halved

200 g (7 oz) small green beans, trimmed

extra virgin olive oil

sea salt and freshly ground black pepper

500-700 g (18-24 oz) fresh tuna

butterleaf lettuce

2 tablespoons capers

4 hardboiled eggs, peeled and halved

4 anchovy fillets

$\frac{1}{4}$ cup niçoise or other good quality olives

a handful of fresh basil leaves, shredded

tuna in seaweed with pickled ginger sauce

I remember being intrigued when I came across this idea. It takes no time to prepare, makes an elegant Japanese-style dish and is equally as good made with salmon fillets.

Preheat the oven to 180°C/350°F.

Combine the garlic with the oil and wasabi and spread onto both sides of each tuna steak. Rinse the seaweed under cold water to soften, and pat dry with a cloth. Spread the seaweed flat on a board, place a tuna steak in the center of each piece and wrap. It may be necessary to cut the tuna steaks in half if they are large. Combine the mirin, water and sesame oil and pour into a baking dish. Add the tuna and bake for about 15 minutes or until it is warmed through, but still pink inside. Remove and keep warm.

Measure $\frac{3}{4}$ cup of cooking liquid, pour into a saucepan, add the ginger and bring to the boil. Stir in the arrowroot mixture and heat until the sauce boils and thickens. Reduce the heat, add the soy sauce, sherry and green onions and simmer for 3 minutes.

To serve, simply cut each package in half. Spoon over the sauce and sprinkle with toasted sesame seeds. Serve with fried noodles.

SERVES 4.

1 clove garlic, crushed

3 teaspoons oil

3 teaspoons wasabi

800 g (28 oz) fresh tuna in one piece, cut into 4 equal slices

4 toasted nori sheets, 20 cm (8") square

$\frac{3}{4}$ cup mirin

$\frac{1}{4}$ cup water

2 teaspoons sesame oil

$\frac{1}{2}$ cup pickled ginger, shredded

2 teaspoons arrowroot blended with 2 teaspoons of water

2 teaspoons light soy sauce

1 tablespoon dry sherry

2 green onions, chopped

2 tablespoons sesame seeds, toasted

meat & poultry

Fast and easy meat dishes call for tender, boneless meat with little fat or sinew. Chicken breasts, beef fillet, lamb cutlets or short loins etc., are cuts that need to be cooked quickly at a high heat, then allowed to rest for several minutes before being sliced. The result: moist, succulent meat.

lamb with orzo and a spiced tomato sauce

Lamb cutlets are one of the quickest cuts of meat to cook. I find myself using them in various guises almost every week. Apart from the barbecue they can be quickly pan fried, grilled or cooked with a grain, as in this orzo dish.

Preheat the oven to 200°C/400°F.

Place the oil in a large, ovenproof sauté pan and heat over a medium-high heat. Season the cutlets with salt and pepper and quickly brown on both sides. Remove, set aside and keep warm.

Reduce the heat and add the onion and garlic. Cook, stirring frequently, until the onion is lightly browned. Increase the heat, add the brandy and cook for 2 minutes. Add the wine and cook a further 2 minutes. Stir in the tomatoes, cinnamon, oregano, allspice, cloves, orange and lemon zest. Simmer for 5 minutes.

Add the chicken stock, zucchini and orzo. Cover and cook for 15 minutes or until the orzo is tender and the liquid is reduced. Taste and season with salt and pepper. Place the lamb cutlets on top of the orzo and place into a hot oven for 5-7 minutes.

To serve, remove the lamb and stir the mint through the orzo. Transfer to a platter and arrange the cutlets on top.

SERVES 4.

2 tablespoons olive oil

12 lamb cutlets

sea salt and freshly ground black pepper

1 cup chopped onion

3 cloves garlic, finely chopped

$\frac{1}{4}$ cup brandy

$\frac{1}{2}$ cup white wine

2 cups canned tomatoes (or 2 x 400g (14 oz) tinned Italian tomatoes)

$\frac{3}{4}$ teaspoon cinnamon

$\frac{3}{4}$ teaspoon dried oregano

$\frac{1}{2}$ teaspoon ground allspice

$\frac{1}{8}$ teaspoon ground cloves

zest of half an orange

zest of half a lemon

$1\frac{1}{2}$ cups chicken stock (see page 196), heated

2 zucchini, cut into large chunks

$1\frac{1}{4}$ cups orzo

2 tablespoons fresh mint, chopped

citrus grilled chicken skewers with honey

We cook a lot of barbecue dishes in our classes. One such dish, a chicken kebab skewered with wedges of lime, has remained a favorite. This grilled chicken was taught at a later date, and since then I have started combining the two. Sometimes I use long, straight rosemary branches with all the leaves removed except for a few at one end. The effect is rustic and the flavors greatly enhanced.

In a small pan, toast the cilantro and aniseed over a moderate heat, tossing, until fragrant. Transfer to a mortar or spice grinder and grind to a powder.

In a bowl, mix together the honey, juices, green onions, thyme, rosemary, sage and ground spice mixture. Add the chicken pieces to the marinade and turn to coat. Allow to marinate, refrigerated for 1-2 hours.

Heat the barbecue or a ridged grill over a moderately high heat.

Remove the chicken from the marinade and season with salt and pepper. Thread the chicken onto metal skewers, occasionally adding a lime wedge. Grill, turning as each side cooks. Brush with the marinade now and again while grilling. Transfer the skewers to a platter to rest before serving.

SERVES 6.

$\frac{1}{2}$ teaspoon cilantro seeds

$\frac{1}{4}$ teaspoon aniseed

$\frac{1}{2}$ cup well-flavored honey

$\frac{1}{4}$ cup fresh lemon juice

3 tablespoons fresh orange juice

3 tablespoons fresh lime juice

2 green onions, finely chopped

1 teaspoon fresh thyme, finely chopped

1 teaspoon rosemary, finely chopped

1 teaspoon sage, finely chopped

12 boneless chicken thighs, cut into large pieces, about 4 cm (1$\frac{1}{2}$") square

sea salt and freshly ground black pepper

1-2 limes, cut into wedges

chicken strips with lemon

A wok can be used, not just for Asian-style stirfries but for many dishes that require fast cooking. This chicken dish is a real five-minute dinner option – perfect for a busy weeknight.

Cut the chicken into thin strips. Heat the stock in a wok and gently poach the chicken strips. Add the green peppercorns, sage and lemon zest. Cook for a few minutes.

Using a slotted spoon, remove the chicken from the pan. Turn up the heat to reduce the stock a little. Add the yogurt and a squeeze of lemon juice. Tip the chicken back into the wok and stir. Taste and season with salt and pepper.

Serve with thick, buttered egg noodles.

SERVES 4.

450 g (1 lb) chicken breast, skin and bones removed

100 ml (3$\frac{1}{2}$ fl oz) chicken or vegetable stock (see page 196)

1$\frac{1}{2}$ teaspoons green peppercorns

2 tablespoons fresh sage leaves, chopped

zest and juice of 1 lemon

3 tablespoons thick, plain, unsweetened yogurt

salt and pepper

ten-minute stroganoff

When I was a young student nurse living in a flat, beef stroganoff was one of my dinner party specials. I wish I'd known this version then, although my budget may not have stretched to the fillet steak needed for this quick cook alternative.

Sprinkle the beef strips generously with the paprika and toss to coat.

Heat the olive oil and butter in a wok over a high heat. Stirfry the beef, along with the green onion, for a couple of minutes. Remove with a slotted spoon and pour out the remaining oil.

Over a low heat, stir the brandy, tomato sauce, lemon juice and sour cream together. Simmer for a minute or two, then tip the beef strips back in and stir together. Season with sea salt and pepper.

Serve over buttered egg noodles or rice.

SERVES 4.

450 g (1 lb) fillet steak, cut into strips

1 tablespoon paprika

1 tablespoon olive oil

knob of butter

2 green onions, finely chopped

1-2 tablespoons brandy

1 teaspoon tomato sauce

squeeze of lemon juice

150 g ($\frac{1}{2}$ cup) sour cream

sea salt and pepper

stir-fried chile pork with cashews

Use the wok for this pork stirfry. Tom Yum Paste will add a delicate lemony note to the dish. It's readily available at Asian stores, as is the Golden Mountain sauce.

fry the cashews in the oil over a medium heat, stirring constantly, until golden brown. Lift out on a slotted spoon and drain on a paper towel. Fry the dried chiles just until they turn dark, then drain them also. Pour off all but 2 tablespoons of oil.

On a high heat, fry the pork until it changes color. Add the curry paste or Tom Yum Paste and fry for a few minutes longer. Add the fish sauce, lime juice, sugar and water and simmer for 10 minutes. Add the Golden Mountain sauce to taste. Thicken the sauce with the cornstarch paste and turn off the heat before adding the fried cashews and chiles.

Serve over rice with lettuce, carrot, cucumber and lime wedges.

SERVES 4.

¼ cup raw cashews

½ cup vegetable oil for frying

6 small dried red chiles

500 g (1 lb) pork fillet, sliced thinly

2 teaspoons red curry paste or Tom Yum Paste

2 tablespoons fish sauce

2 tablespoons lime juice

1 teaspoon brown sugar

½ cup water

2 teaspoons Golden Mountain sauce

1 teaspoon cornstarch mixed with a little water

lamb, eggplant and orzo salad

This is a good dish when you have leftover barbecued or even roast lamb. It's a perfect match with the orzo and the lemony, garlic dressing. Orzo is one of the most versatile 'grains'. It takes the place of rice or beans but, because it's pasta, takes only a fraction of the time to cook.

Preheat the oven to 190°C/375°F. Place the eggplant in a baking pan. Drizzle with the olive oil, add the garlic and toss to combine. Bake, stirring occasionally, until the eggplant is tender – 30-40 minutes. Allow to cool.

Cook the orzo till al dente in abundant boiling, salted water, then drain and cool under running water.

Combine with the lamb, olives, red onion, pepper, tomatoes, pinenuts, parsley and rosemary in a large mixing bowl. Add the eggplant and toss all the ingredients together well.

To prepare the dressing, place the egg, egg yolk, lemon juice, oregano, garlic and lemon zest in a food processor fitted with the steel blade. Process for 10 seconds. With the machine running, pour the oil in a thin, steady stream through the feed tube to make a thick mayonnaise. Season to taste with salt and pepper.

Bind the salad with the dressing and transfer to a serving bowl. Garnish with fresh sprigs of rosemary. Serve slightly chilled or at room temperature.

SERVES 6-8.

1 large eggplant, cut into chunks

$\frac{1}{2}$ cup olive oil

2 cloves garlic

500 g (1 lb) orzo

500 g (1 lb) rare cooked lamb, sliced

$\frac{3}{4}$ cup pitted Kalamata olives, cut in half

$\frac{1}{2}$ red onion, finely chopped

1 yellow bell pepper, cut into $1\frac{1}{2}$ cm ($\frac{1}{2}$") dice

$\frac{1}{2}$ cup red or yellow cherry tomatoes, quartered

$\frac{1}{4}$ cup pinenuts, toasted

$\frac{1}{2}$ bunch fresh parsley, finely chopped

$1\frac{1}{2}$ tablespoons rosemary, finely chopped

DRESSING

1 whole egg

1 egg yolk

2 tablespoons lemon juice

1 teaspoon dried oregano

3 cloves garlic, finely chopped

1 teaspoon finely grated lemon zest

$1\frac{1}{4}$ cups olive oil

salt and freshly ground black pepper to taste

sprigs of rosemary to garnish

117

paillard of beef with watercress, olives and tomatoes

This is one of the fastest beef dishes I know, but it is entirely dependent on using a very good cut of meat. Fillet is the only beef cut that can be cooked so quickly and still be tender and succulent. However, chicken breasts or lamb fillets can also be prepared and cooked in the same way and are equally good in this dish.

Slice the fillet 6 mm ($\frac{1}{4}$") inch thick, place each slice between plastic wrap and flatten with a rolling pin. Brush each piece with olive oil. These can be prepared ahead, covered and refrigerated until needed.

Combine the olives, tomatoes, oregano, salt and pepper in a bowl and set aside at room temperature.

Line a serving platter with the watercress or arugula.

Heat a cast-iron grill or frypan and oil lightly. Sear the beef quickly, so it is still pink in the middle, removing immediately to the platter as each piece is cooked. Season. Spoon over the olive and tomato mixture, drizzle with olive oil and serve.

SERVES 6-8.

1-1$\frac{1}{4}$ kg (2$\frac{3}{4}$ lb) beef fillet, trimmed of all sinew, backstrap removed

extra virgin olive oil

$\frac{1}{2}$ cup Kalamata olives, pitted and quartered

2 large ripe, red tomatoes, diced

1 bunch fresh oregano leaves, coarsely chopped

sea salt and freshly ground black pepper

2-3 bunches watercress, or baby arugula, washed

creamy polenta with lamb and red wine sauce

Donna Hay, food editor of Australia's Marie Claire *magazine, was a guest at our cookschool in 1998. Her books are amongst some of the most popular we have ever sold. This polenta and lamb combination, adapted from her first book* Marie Claire Cooking, *is the sort of food that warms and comforts you with the first mouthful. We use Maggie Beer's quince paste but, if unavailable, it could be substituted with redcurrant jelly. Likewise replace the mascarpone with another $\frac{1}{2}$ cup of cream.*

Place the chicken stock, cream and garlic in a large pot and heat until boiling. Add the Parmesan and slowly pour in the polenta and semolina, whisking to combine. Cook over a low temperature for 20 minutes. Add the mascarpone and season well with salt and pepper.

Preheat the oven to 200°C/400°F.

Place a heavy frypan over a high heat. Brush the lamb with olive oil and season with salt and pepper. Sear the lamb quickly on all sides until it is well browned. Remove from the pan and place on a baking tray. Transfer to the oven and cook until the lamb is medium rare – 7-10 minutes depending on thickness. Remove the meat from oven and allow to rest for 5 minutes before slicing.

Add the wine, stock and quince paste to the pan and simmer for 5 minutes or until the sauce has thickened. Taste and season.

To serve, place the polenta on a serving platter, top with sliced lamb and spoon over the sauce. Serve immediately.

SERVES 4.

300-400 g (11-14 oz) lamb striploin, trimmed
olive oil to brush
salt and freshly ground black pepper
$\frac{3}{4}$ cup red wine
$\frac{3}{4}$ cup beef stock
3 tablespoons quince paste

CREAMY POLENTA
2 liters (8 cups) chicken stock (see page 196)
$\frac{1}{2}$ cup cream
2 teaspoons crushed garlic
$\frac{1}{2}$ cup Parmesan cheese, freshly grated
$\frac{3}{4}$ cup fine polenta
1 cup semolina
$\frac{1}{2}$ cup mascarpone
salt and freshly ground black pepper

kashmiri lamb koftas
in saffron sauce

Charmaine Solomon has been a constant source of inspiration to me since I first started cooking. Her name is synonymous with Asian cooking. This lamb dish is adapted from one in Charmaine's Encyclopedia of Asian Food.

roughly chop the lamb into cubes and process in a food processor, a quarter at a time, until a smooth paste is formed. Mix the garam masala, salt and arrowroot with the water until smooth. Add to the meat. Using wet hands, form the meat paste into ovals the size of a small egg. Poach in a saucepan with 5 cm (2") lightly salted boiling water, with half the turmeric and chile powder for 10 minutes.

Heat the ghee and fry the onion, ginger and whole spices until the onion is soft and golden. Stir in the remaining turmeric and chile powder along with the paprika and tomato paste. Add the meatballs with some of their cooking liquid. Cover and simmer until tender – about 30 minutes. Lightly toast the saffron strands in a dry pan, crush to a dry powder and dissolve in the boiling water. Stir in towards the end of cooking and garnish with cilantro. Serve with rice and vegetables.

SERVES 6.

750 g (26 oz) boneless lamb

1½ teaspoons garam masala

1 teaspoon salt

3 tablespoons arrowroot

2 tablespoons cold water

1 teaspoon turmeric

1-2 teaspoons chile powder, or to taste

2 tablespoons ghee (clarified butter)

1 medium onion, sliced finely

2 teaspoons fresh ginger, finely chopped

1 small stick of cinnamon

4 whole cloves

3 cardamom pods, bruised

2 teaspoons paprika

2 teaspoons tomato paste

¼ teaspoon saffron threads

2 tablespoons boiling water

2 tablespoons fresh cilantro, finely chopped

rabbit with mushrooms and thyme

This is a traditional French bistro dish that I have cooked for years. One of my most memorable meals of rabbit was enjoyed in a house set amongst vineyards. Needless to say the rabbits we ate had, not long before, been dining on choice vine shoots near the house. This dish comes from another favorite book of mine, Bistro *by Patricia Wells. Farmed rabbits are readily available to order from butchers or you could use chicken instead.*

Season the rabbit pieces liberally with salt and pepper. Heat the oil in a deep-sided frypan over a medium-high heat. When the oil is hot, add the rabbit and turn the pieces until all are well browned.

Remove the rabbit to a dish. Add the onion, bacon and mushrooms and brown in the fat for 3-4 minutes. Add the wine, carefully, as it will bubble and spit as it hits the hot pan. Add the rabbit and bayleaves. Cover, reduce the heat to medium and cook until the rabbit is tender – about 20 minutes.

Remove the rabbit to a warm platter. Cover and keep warm.

Combine the rabbit/chicken liver, mustard, thyme leaves and breadcrumbs in a food processor. Process until smooth. Stir the mixture into the sauce remaining in the pan. Taste and season if required with salt and pepper. Pour over the rabbit and serve.

SERVES 4.

1 fresh rabbit, about 1½ kg (3½ lb), cut into 7 or 8 serving pieces, liver reserved (or use a chicken liver)

salt and freshly ground black pepper

3 tablespoons extra virgin olive oil

2 medium onions, coarsely chopped

140 g (5 oz) bacon, diced

250 g (9 oz) button mushrooms, thinly sliced

625 ml (2½ cups) dry white wine

4 bayleaves and a sprig of thyme, tied with string

3 tablespoons Dijon mustard

⅓ cup fresh thyme leaves

½ cup fresh breadcrumbs

chicken and spinach phyllo pie

I asked Nan Greville, a friend who has been coming to 'Gourmet on the Run' since its inception, what her all-time favorite dish was from the collection. This pie topped quite a long list. It is delicious served with a green salad and some crusty bread. You could also make individual little pies using 12 cm (5") loose-bottomed tart pans.

Toss the chicken strips with a little olive oil, oregano, salt and pepper. Heat a heavy pan over a medium-high heat and quickly fry the chicken until cooked. Remove from the pan and set aside.

In a small saucepan, heat the cream to almost boiling and keep warm.

Melt $\frac{1}{4}$ cup butter in the chicken pan over a medium heat. Add the onion and sauté until translucent. Add the garlic and cook for 2 minutes. Add the spinach and cook, stirring often, until wilted – about 3 minutes. Add the flour and stir well to blend. Simmer for 2 minutes, then add the warm cream and bring to the boil. Reduce the heat to low and stir in the nutmeg and salt and pepper to taste.

Preheat the oven to 200°C/400°F.

Butter the inside of a pie dish or cake pan with melted butter. Take 1 sheet of phyllo and lightly butter it. Cover with another sheet and place in the pie tin. Continue with 3 more buttered doubles of phyllo and angle around so that the bottom and sides are covered with pastry. Spoon about half of the spinach mixture onto the bottom of the pastry. Cover the mixture with the cooked chicken strips. Top with the remaining spinach mixture and sprinkle with the crumbled feta.

Fold phyllo sheets back over the pie mixture so that it is completely covered. Brush top with melted butter and bake in preheated oven for 10-15 minutes until the phyllo starts to cook. At this stage scrunched sheets of buttered phyllo can be added on top to decorate, then cook for a further 10 minutes until crisp and lightly browned.

Remove to a platter and serve hot.

SERVES 4.

5-6 boneless chicken breasts, skinned
and sliced $2\frac{1}{2}$ cm (1") thick

olive oil

2 tablespoons fresh oregano, chopped,
or 1 tablespoon dried

salt and pepper

1 cup cream

$\frac{1}{4}$ cup unsalted butter

1 onion, finely chopped

3 cloves garlic, finely chopped

250 g (9 oz) spinach, shredded $2\frac{1}{2}$ cm
(1") wide

$2\frac{1}{2}$ tablespoons flour

$\frac{1}{2}$ teaspoon freshly grated nutmeg

10-12 sheets of phyllo dough

$\frac{1}{4}$ cup unsalted butter, melted, for
brushing phyllo

150 g (5 $\frac{1}{2}$ oz) feta cheese, crumbled

saucy chicken and arugula meatballs

The concept of meatballs has never thrilled me, probably because in my very first cooking job I had to roll hundreds and hundreds of cocktail-sized ones. However, these chicken and arugula meatballs are enhanced with so many interesting ingredients and taste so good that I do enjoy both making and eating them.

In a large skillet, heat the olive oil. Add the bacon and cook until crisp. Add the garlic and cook, stirring, until fragrant. Add the arugula and cook, stirring, until wilted. Transfer to a plate and let cool.

In a large bowl, combine the chicken, breadcrumbs, cheese, capers, egg, salt and pepper. Add the arugula mixture and blend well. Roll the mixture into 2 cm (¾") balls.

In a large frypan, heat enough olive oil to cover the base of the pan. Add as many meatballs as will fit in a single layer and cook over a moderate heat, turning until browned all over. Using a slotted spoon, transfer the meatballs to a large plate. Repeat with any remaining meatballs. Discard the fat and wipe out the skillet.

In the same skillet, melt the butter over a moderate heat. Add the shallots and cook until softened – about 3 minutes. Add the cognac, raise the heat to high and cook until evaporated. Add the tomatoes and thyme and season with salt and pepper. Bring to a simmer and cook until the sauce is thick – about 8 minutes. Add the meatballs to the sauce and simmer over a low heat just until heated through. Serve immediately.

SERVES 4.

2 tablespoons olive oil, plus extra for frying
80 g (3 oz) bacon, chopped
2 cloves garlic, finely chopped
150 g (5 oz) arugula leaves, finely chopped
450 g (1 lb) minced chicken
½ cup plus 2 tablespoons plain dry breadcrumbs
½ cup freshly grated Pecorino Romano cheese
2 tablespoons drained capers, chopped
1 large egg, lightly beaten
salt and freshly ground black pepper

SAUCE
3 tablespoons unsalted butter
2 shallots, finely chopped
¼ cup brandy or cognac
1 kg (2 lb) canned tomatoes in juice, coarsely chopped in food processor
1 teaspoon fresh thyme, finely chopped
salt and freshly ground black pepper

cilantro chile rice with chicken

At first glance you may think this dish is searingly hot. On the contrary, it has a pleasant zing. However, you can adjust the amount of chile to your liking. Charring the chiles gives them a delectable smoky flavor, which is the secret to this dish.

thoroughly char the chiles over a gas burner or place under a hot grill. Place the blackened chiles into a container, cover tightly and let them steam for 10 minutes. Scrape off the blackened skin and remove the stems, seeds and veins. Set 1 chile aside for garnish.

Place the chiles in a blender with the onion, garlic, cilantro, lime juice and water. Purée until the sauce is smooth.

Rinse the rice under running water in a large sieve until the water runs clear. Set aside to drain well.

Heat the olive oil in a large, heavy casserole with a tight-fitting lid. Brown the chicken pieces over a medium heat until golden brown – about 10 minutes each side. Remove to a plate to drain. Lower the heat and sauté the rice until opaque – about 2 minutes – scraping up some of the browned bits from the bottom of the pan. Add the chile-onion purée and cook until aromatic. Add the chicken pieces and $2\frac{1}{2}$ cups of chicken stock. Stir well and bring to the boil. Reduce the heat to medium low and cook uncovered for 10 minutes. Cover tightly and cook over a low heat until the chicken and rice are tender and the liquid is absorbed – about 20 minutes. Add the reserved stock if the rice gets too dry.

Remove the casserole from the heat and place a double layer of paper towels under the lid to absorb the steam. Allow to rest for 10 minutes.

Chop the reserved chile and sprinkle it over the dish with the cilantro to garnish.

SERVES 4-6.

6 mild long green chiles, such as
   Anaheim's
1 onion, coarsely chopped
3 cloves garlic, chopped
1 bunch cilantro, stems removed
juice of 1 lime
$\frac{1}{2}$ cup water
2 cups long grain white rice
3 tablespoons olive oil
8 boned chicken thighs, skin on, cut
   into large pieces
3 cups chicken stock (see page 196)
salt and pepper to taste
fresh cilantro to garnish

salads

herbed orzo with asparagus, chickpeas and feta dressing

These days I tend to cheat a little when I need chickpeas and purchase them, ready cooked, in cans. However, if these are not available, soak the dried chickpeas overnight, drain, cover with fresh water and simmer gently until tender. Alternatively, use a pressure cooker and they'll be ready in 15-20 minutes.

Preheat the oven to 150°C/300°F.

Line a baking tray with a nonstick sheet. Place the tomatoes on the tray, cut side up. Brush the tops lightly with olive oil and season with salt and pepper. Cook for 1 hour or until the tomatoes are starting to dry out and the edges have shrivelled.

Bring a large pot of water to a rolling boil. Salt the water and cook the orzo until al dente – 10-15 minutes. Drain and cool under cold water to halt cooking. Set aside in a strainer.

Combine the chickpeas and half the chives in a large bowl. Set aside.

In a blender, place lemon juice, pepper, feta and oil. Blend until creamy. Combine orzo and chickpeas and pour over feta dressing. Add remaining chives and toss well to combine. Season well with salt and pepper.

Place the asparagus and salad on a platter, and scatter the tomatoes over the top. Garnish with lemon wedges.

SERVES 8.

1 basket cherry tomatoes, cut in half

olive oil to brush

salt and fresh ground black pepper

2 cups uncooked orzo (makes about 5 cups)

2 cups cooked chickpeas

half a bunch of chives, chopped into 5 cm (2") lengths

$\frac{1}{4}$ cup freshly squeezed lemon juice

50 g (1$\frac{3}{4}$ oz) feta cheese

3 tablespoons extra virgin olive oil

1 kg (2 lb) asparagus, blanched

lemon wedges, to garnish

vietnamese minted lemon beef salad

There's an amazing Japanese tool called a Benriner slicer that many cooks, both professional and at home, wouldn't be without. It will julienne or slice all the vegetables for salads such as this one in next to no time. The Vietnamese flavors here are fresh and alive. It's a good barbecue number because you can have the salad ready and the beef marinating. Just toss it on the hotplate for a few minutes and it's done.

Marinate the beef with the cayenne, 2 teaspoons of the brown sugar and 1½ tablespoons of the fish sauce for at least 30 minutes. Preheat the grill or barbecue until very hot. Sear the beef on all sides so it is still pink in the center. Remove to a plate and rest.

Using a mortar and pestle or a small food processor, crush the chile, ginger and garlic to a paste with the salt. Add the lemon juice and remaining fish sauce, sugar and hot water. Stir well to dissolve the sugar. Cut the beef into thin slices, place in a bowl with the lemon slices and 2 tablespoons of the dressing. Set aside until needed or cover and refrigerate overnight.

To make the salad, mix all the ingredients well in a large bowl. Toss with the remaining dressing. Arrange the salad on a large platter, scatter the meat on top. Sprinkle over the peanuts and serve.

SERVES 4-6.

500 g (1lb) sirloin or other tender steak

¼ teaspoon cayenne pepper

2½ tablespoons light brown sugar

5 tablespoons fish sauce

1 small hot chile, stem removed and chopped

1½ teaspoons grated ginger

1 large clove garlic

½ teaspoon salt

7 tablespoons fresh lemon juice

2 tablespoons hot water

2 lemons, skin and pith removed, sliced thinly

SALAD

1 cup carrots, julienned

2 medium cucumbers, peeled, seeded and julienned

½ small red onion, halved, sliced very thin, rings separated

2½ cups red or green cabbage, shredded

1 cup bean sprouts

2 large handfuls mint leaves, shredded

handful basil leaves, shredded

salt to taste

⅓ cup roasted peanuts

eggplant with pomegranate sauce

My first encounter with pomegranates came long before my cooking days began. As a young student nurse in the '70s I got to know a very homesick patient, newly arrived from Lebanon. Beside her bed was a bowl of these beautiful ruby fruit. They were, she said, one of the few culinary links she had with her homeland and she broke one open and allowed me to taste the brilliant beads of fruit that nestled inside.

Although pomegranates do grow in New Zealand, the fruit rarely ripens fully, so look for imported fruit that appear occasionally over the summer. Pomegranate molasses is the result of long slow boiling of pomegranate juice. Available in bottles, it has an intense sweet/sour flavor that I find quite irresistible. This eggplant dish comes from Paula Wolfert's book, The Cooking of the Eastern Mediterranean.

Preheat the oven to 210°C/425°F.

Slice the eggplant on the diagonal into 1.25 cm (½") thick slices. Spread onto a baking sheet and brush with olive oil. Bake for 12-15 minutes on each side until golden.

Place the slices in a shallow serving dish.

Combine the pomegranate molasses, lemon juice, garlic, sugar, olive oil and salt. Drizzle over the eggplant. Sprinkle over the mint and parsley and pomegranate seeds if available. Cover and let stand until ready to serve or refrigerate overnight.

SERVES 6.

750 g (26 oz) eggplant
olive oil

SAUCE
2 tablespoons pomegranate molasses
1 tablespoon fresh lemon juice
1 small clove garlic, crushed to a paste
  with salt
¼ teaspoon sugar
1½ tablespoons olive oil
½ teaspoon sea salt
2-3 tablespoons fresh mint, chopped
1 tablespoon flat-leaf parsley, chopped
2 tablespoons fresh pomegranate seeds
  (optional)

wilted spinach salad
with roasted bell pepper

Roasting peppers not only enables the easy removal of the bitter skin but also intensifies the sweetness of the flesh. When roasted in the oven they become very soft, so, if you prefer them al dente, char them over a gas flame instead. This salad may seem unusual at first glance, but it is quite delicious. The hot olive oil initially wilts the spinach then cleverly becomes the dressing.

Preheat the oven to 200°C/400° F.

Roast the bell pepper in the hot oven until the skin is black and blistered. Alternatively, hold over a gas flame until the skin is charred. Wrap in a teatowel for a few minutes until cool enough to handle. Peel off the charred skin and remove the core and seeds. Reduce the oven temperature to 180°C/350°F.

Slice the pepper into strips, toss with ½ tablespoon of olive oil, salt and pepper and set aside to marinate. Cover the onion slices with cold water to leach out their strong flavor.

Place the French bread slices on a baking tray and brush lightly with olive oil. Toast them until crisp and lightly browned. Remove from the oven and rub each crouton with a peeled garlic clove. Set aside.

In a large bowl combine the vinegar, the chopped garlic and ½ teaspoon of salt and a few grinds of pepper. Add the greens, basil, onion, pepper and olives. Be sure to include the sweet juice of the pepper, as it will add flavor to the salad.

Heat the remaining ¼ cup of oil in a small skillet until it is very hot. Immediately pour it over the salad and toss to coat and wilt the leaves, sprinkling in the Parmesan as you toss. Add the croutons and pinenuts and serve immediately.

SERVES 4-6.

1 large red or yellow bell pepper

6 tablespoons olive oil

salt and pepper

½ red onion, thinly sliced

8-12 thin slices of French bread for croutons

3 tablespoons balsamic vinegar

2 cloves garlic (finely chop 1 clove)

1-2 bunches of spinach, washed well, stems removed

2 small bunches of frisée lettuce, washed

handful of fresh basil

10 black olives, pitted

⅓ cup freshly grated Parmesan cheese

2 tablespoons roasted pinenuts (optional)

jersey bennes with bacon and cayenne-toasted pecans

Just like asparagus, Jersey Benne potatoes are one of the year's culinary highlights for me. The short season begins in October/November and is over quickly because these exquisite potatoes don't store through the winter months. In fact they need to be eaten as soon as possible after being dug. You'll recognize them in their attractive boxes, necessary to protect them from bruising and daylight.

Preheat the oven to 180°C/350°F.

Toss the pecans, salt, cayenne and butter together in a small bowl. Spread out onto a baking sheet and toast, watching carefully, until golden – about 10 minutes. Set aside to cool.

Cut the cooked potatoes in half lengthways or slice, depending on their size.

Sauté the bacon until crisp and drain on paper towels, leaving the bacon fat in the pan. When bacon is cool, chop into pieces. Pour all but 2 teaspoons of the bacon fat out of the pan. Add the green onion and sauté until softened. Remove the pan from the heat and whisk in the sherry, vinegar, mustard seeds, honey and parsley. Combine well. Whisk in the oil in a slow stream.

Pour the dressing over the warm potatoes, sprinkle in the bacon and toss gently to coat well. At this stage the salad can be left for an hour for the flavors to develop. Toss in the pecans, taste and season if necessary.

SERVES 6.

$\frac{1}{2}$ *cup pecan pieces*

$\frac{1}{4}$ *teaspoon sea salt*

$\frac{1}{8}$ *teaspoon cayenne*

1 teaspoon unsalted butter, melted

1 kg (2 lb) Jersey Bennes or waxy red potatoes, cooked whole until tender

6 strips bacon

$\frac{1}{2}$ *cup very finely chopped green onion*

$\frac{1}{4}$ *cup dry sherry*

$\frac{1}{4}$ *cup apple-cider vinegar*

1 teaspoon mustard seeds

1 tablespoon honey

2 large sprigs flat-leaf parsley, finely chopped

$\frac{1}{2}$ *cup canola or olive oil*

sea salt and freshly ground black pepper

parsley and grilled vegetable salad

Grilled vegetables are wonderful on their own, but even better combined with parsley and this caper and olive dressing. Semi-dried tomatoes are available from delicatessens, or it is possible to make your own. Simply cut some tomatoes in half, sprinkle with salt and leave to drain upside down on paper towels for 30 minutes. Place on a baking tray in a 150°C/300°F oven and bake slowly until the tomato starts to shrivel a little. You'll find that the flavor will have intensified. Cool, refrigerate and use within a couple of days.

Preheat a barbecue or ridged grill.

Pick over the parsley, remove from the stalks, wash and dry well.

Smash and finely chop the garlic. Mix with the olive oil and salt and pepper, and set aside to infuse.

Cut the eggplants across and the zucchini lengthways into 5 mm (¼") slices. Halve and seed the peppers; trim the green onions.

Brush the vegetables with garlic oil and grill until cooked and well colored. Set aside.

Brush the slices of bread with garlic oil and grill until crisp and golden.

Place the grilled bread into a food processor and process to a fine crumb.

To make the dressing, chop the capers, olives, onion, garlic and tomatoes with a large knife. Place into a salad bowl with the oil and vinegar, adjust the seasoning and stir.

Mix all the grilled vegetables together in a large serving bowl. Add the parsley to the dressing and toss, then add to the vegetables and mix thoroughly. Scatter the top with a thin layer of crumbs.

SERVES 4-6.

1 large bunch of flat-leaf parsley

2 cloves garlic

4 tablespoons olive oil

salt and pepper

2 medium eggplants

2 large zucchini

1 red bell pepper

1 yellow bell pepper

8 green onions

1-2 thick slices of country style bread

DRESSING

1 tablespoon capers, drained

16 black olives, pitted

½ cup red onion

1 clove garlic

4 semi-dried tomatoes

150 ml (10 tablespoons) extra virgin olive oil

2-3 tablespoons balsamic vinegar

chinese noodle salad
with citrus and spicy peanuts

Throughout this book I frequently sing the praises of Asian noodles for their versatility and fast preparation time. These fresh noodles take a little longer in that they are cooked in a similar way to Italian pasta. A Benriner slicer (see page 9) will make light work of the vegetable preparation.

Using a zesting tool, remove the zest from the orange. Set aside to add to the salad later. Combine all of the remaining marinade ingredients in a blender and purée. Set aside $\frac{1}{2}$ cup of the marinade to toss with the vegetable garnish.

Bring a large pot of water to the boil. Add salt and drop the carrot and snow peas into the water and cook for about 30 seconds. Scoop them out and refresh under cold water. Set aside.

Separate and fluff the noodles so they don't stick together while they are cooking. Drop them into the boiling water, give them a quick stir and cook for 3-4 minutes. Remove from the water when they are just tender. Drain and then refresh with cold water.

Toss the snow peas, carrot, green onions and radish together in a small bowl. Add half the vegetables to the noodles and toss with the marinade, ginger, orange threads, cilantro and chile flakes. Toss the remaining vegetables with the reserved marinade and arrange on top of the noodles. Garnish the salad with spicy peanuts and sprigs of cilantro.

SERVES 6-8.

MARINADE

zest of 1 orange

$\frac{1}{2}$ cup fresh orange juice

$2\frac{1}{2}$ tablespoons grated ginger

3 tablespoons rice wine vinegar

5 tablespoons soy sauce

3 tablespoons sherry vinegar

$\frac{1}{2}$ cup sesame oil

$1\frac{1}{2}$ tablespoons sugar

SALAD

sea salt

1 medium carrot, cut into fine julienne

60 g (2 oz) snow peas, strings removed and cut into julienne

400 g (14 oz) package fresh thin Chinese noodles or angel hair pasta

2 green onions, both green and white part, thinly sliced on the diagonal

$\frac{1}{2}$ cup daikon radish, cut into julienne

5 cm (2") piece of fresh ginger, peeled and cut into julienne

good handful chopped cilantro and sprigs for garnish

1 teaspoon chile flakes

$\frac{1}{2}$ cup spicy peanuts

tuscan salad

The Tuscans are famous for their bread salads. It's just one of the ways they have devised to use up their bread, which, because it contains no salt, goes stale very quickly. This is a modern variation – in fact we use French bread here, not Italian. Try it, it's sensational!

break the French bread into pieces, place in a roasting pan and sprinkle with olive oil. Bake until golden brown and crunchy.

Combine all the ingredients in a large bowl and toss with a vinaigrette made with the extra virgin olive oil, balsamic vinegar and salt.

Arrange on a large platter and using a vegetable peeler shave Parmesan over the top to garnish.

SERVES 4-6.

1 loaf of French bread

olive oil

12 large green stuffed olives

5 tomatoes, chopped roughly

1 cucumber, chopped roughly

2 red onions, sliced thinly

2 red radicchio, leaves torn roughly

12 caper berries

6 gherkins, chopped

4 sprigs of flat-leaf parsley, chopped coarsely

1 fennel bulb, thinly sliced

125 ml (8 tablespoons) extra virgin olive oil

1-2 tablespoons balsamic vinegar

sea salt

fresh Parmesan cheese in a piece

warm potato and mussel salad

This is easy! Simply cook the mussels and potatoes and combine in a saffron sauce. Another way to celebrate two fabulous ingredients. Try to buy the mussels on the day you want to cook them. When you get them home, remove them from the plastic bag and place in a bowl. Cover with wet paper towels and refrigerate. When you come to prepare them, as close as possible to cooking, scrub or scrape them clean and pull off the 'beard'. Discard any with broken shells.

Heat the olive oil in a large pot. Add the garlic and sauté until lightly colored. Add the white wine, peppercorns, parsley and the mussels, cover and turn up the heat. Shake the pan after several minutes of cooking and remove any mussels that have opened. Continue shaking the pan over the heat and removing the mussels as they open, discarding any that remain closed. Strain the juice through a fine strainer, or wet muslin cloth and reserve.

Meanwhile, cook the potatoes in boiling, salted water until they are tender, but still firm. Drain and slice them into 1 cm ($\frac{1}{3}$") slices. Coat the potatoes in olive oil, lemon juice and pepper.

Arrange the potatoes and the mussels together on serving plates. Heat the reserved mussel juice and saffron in a small pan. Whisk in the butter until the sauce is frothy and pour it over the salad.

Scatter the herbs over the top and serve with crusty bread.

SERVES 6.

2 tablespoons extra virgin olive oil

2 cloves garlic, finely chopped

1 cup white wine

6 black peppercorns

4 stalks of parsley

2 kg (4$\frac{1}{2}$ lb) small, fresh green-lip mussels, scrubbed clean and bearded

1 kg (2 lb) waxy red-skinned potatoes or Jersey Bennes

juice of 1 lemon

freshly ground black pepper

pinch saffron threads – toasted and crushed

1 tablespoon butter, cut into cubes

1 tablespoon chervil or parsley, finely chopped

vegetables

gratin of eggplant with tomato and basil vinaigrette

The three main ingredients here are just made to go together. I can happily eat this gratin for lunch with a piece of crusty bread or serve it alongside grilled lamb, chicken or fish. This dish tastes as good as it looks!

Preheat the oven to 180°C/350°F.

Season the eggplant and dredge very lightly with flour. Heat $\frac{1}{4}$ cup of oil in a large nonstick frypan over a medium heat. Add the eggplant slices and sauté until browned on both sides. Drain on paper towels. Continue to sauté the remaining eggplant, adding more oil to the pan as necessary.

Transfer the eggplant to a baking dish, layering it with tomato and sliced garlic. Season with salt and pepper. Bake for 10-15 minutes or until tomatoes are heated through.

To make the vinaigrette, purée the basil, crushed garlic and two vinegars in a blender. Add 6 tablespoons of olive oil, taste and season with salt and pepper.

Sprinkle the breadcrumbs and parsley over the warm gratin and drizzle with the basil vinaigrette. Serve warm or at room temperature.

SERVES 6 AS A VEGETABLE DISH.

2 medium eggplants or 5 long Japanese eggplants, sliced 1.25 cm ($\frac{1}{2}$") thick

flour

olive oil

2 medium tomatoes, sliced

2 large garlic cloves, thinly sliced

sea salt and black pepper

1 cup fresh basil leaves

1 garlic clove, crushed

2 teaspoons red wine vinegar

$2\frac{1}{2}$ teaspoons balsamic vinegar

$\frac{1}{2}$ cup fresh breadcrumbs, fried in a little olive oil until crisp

2 tablespoons flat-leaf parsley, chopped

pumpkin gratin

In Italy with Maggie Beer and Stephanie Alexander, we picked pumpkins of varying shapes and sizes from the garden to make this gratin. I can't be sure if it was the sun or the glass of Moscato d'Asti I had before lunch, but I have never tasted pumpkin so good. Although it has never tasted quite as good again, it's still one of the nicest ways I've found to prepare pumpkin.

Preheat the oven to 180°C/350°F.

Put ¼ cup olive oil, some pepper and a few flakes of sea salt into a large bowl, then stir in the Parmesan. Toss the pumpkin with this mixture until well coated.

Choose a shallow gratin dish into which the pumpkin will fit snugly and brush with olive oil.

Pile in the pumpkin and bake for 45 minutes to 1 hour. If the cheese browns before the pumpkin is tender, cover the dish with tinfoil for the last 15 minutes of cooking.

SERVES 6.

extra virgin olive oil

freshly ground black pepper

sea salt

3 tablespoons freshly grated Parmesan cheese

1 kg (2 lb) peeled pumpkin, cut into 3 cm (1¼") chunks

brussels sprouts with walnuts, balsamic vinegar and mint

I knew no-one would believe I was going to cook Brussels sprouts in class. However, that most disliked of vegetables was taken to new heights with this simple but delicious recipe. I have a feeling there were a few converts that week and that sales of Brussels sprouts soared at stores nearby!

In a pot of boiling, salted water, cook the Brussels sprouts until bright green and almost tender – about 6 minutes. Drain and immediately plunge the Brussels sprouts into ice water to stop the cooking. Pat dry with paper towels.

In a large sauté pan, melt the butter over a high heat until it begins to brown. Add the Brussels sprouts in an even layer and cook without stirring until they brown on the bottom – about 8 minutes.

Add the vinegar and cook, stirring, until the vinegar reduces and glazes the Brussels sprouts – about 3 minutes.

Season with salt and pepper, stir in the walnuts and mint and serve at once.

SERVES 4-6.

1 kg (2 lb) small Brussels sprouts, trimmed and scored on the bottom

2 teaspoons unsalted butter

1-2 teaspoons balsamic vinegar

salt and fresh ground black pepper

$\frac{1}{4}$ cup walnuts, toasted

2 tablespoons chopped mint

zucchini with basil and
pecorino romano cheese

In the farmers' markets in the USA I sometimes see green and yellow zucchini the size of my little finger and am always disappointed that I can't buy some to cook. I would prepare them whole exactly this way. Small zucchini will always be sweeter, so pick them out especially for this dish.

Wash the zucchini and slice into thin disks.

Place the olive oil in a large sauté pan and turn the heat to high. Throw in the zucchini and toss in the oil until the slices are lightly colored but still crisp. Turn the heat to medium low, add the garlic and season with salt and pepper to taste. Cook until the zucchini are tender but still have a trace of crispness.

Pile onto a serving platter, sprinkle with grated Pecorino Romano and shredded fresh basil leaves.

SERVES 6-8.

700 g (1½ lb) small zucchini

4 tablespoons olive oil

3 garlic cloves, chopped

salt and black pepper to taste

3 tablespoons freshly grated Pecorino Romano cheese

handful of small basil leaves

baked vegetables with citrus

The first time I ate something cooked en papillote *I was about 17 and in a very fancy restaurant in New Orleans. I can still remember the aroma that met me when the waiter opened the package at the table. This dish will have the same effect for you. It's a perfect winter vegetable dish to serve with any simply cooked meat, or on its own with some crusty bread to soak up the sauce. To cook the chestnuts, make a cross in the top, boil or steam, then peel with a small sharp knife. The yams used here are the small red or yellow variety with a very uneven surface.*

Preheat the oven to 200°C/400°F.

Cut tinfoil or baking paper into six 30 cm (12") squares, and turn up the edges to form bowl-shaped containers.

Melt half the butter in a medium frypan and sauté the garlic, onions and carrots over a medium heat until lightly browned.

Add the parsnips, turnips, pumpkin, yams and thyme and sauté for 2-3 minutes more. With a slotted spoon, transfer the vegetables to the prepared foil containers. Add the remaining butter and orange zest to the pan, pour in the brandy, orange juice, stock and add the honey. Bring to a boil and cook over a high heat until reduced to about 6 tablespoons.

Spoon a tablespoon into each foil container and add the chestnuts and seasoning.

Pull the edges of the foil together and turn them over or tie to seal in the vegetables and their juices completely. Place in a large baking pan and bake for 20 minutes. Remove the packets from the oven and serve straight from the foil or transfer to serving plates. The garlic, now soft and caramelized can be easily squeezed from their skins and eaten.

SERVES 6.

50 g (3 tablespoons) unsalted butter

12 cloves garlic, unpeeled

a selection of the following vegetables:
  baby red onions or shallots, carrots,
  parsnips, turnips, pumpkin, yams

sprigs of thyme

orange zest

2 tablespoons brandy

$\frac{1}{2}$ cup orange juice

$\frac{1}{2}$ cup vegetable stock or water

1 tablespoon honey

1 cup cooked chestnuts (optional)

salt and freshly ground black pepper

stirfried sesame cabbage with ginger

For cabbage to be tasty and appealing it needs to be either raw or just wilted and still a little crisp. Gone are the days when it was boiled and boiled until it was lifeless. The simple Asian flavors used here have an amazing effect on a vegetable that many view as tasteless and boring.

heat the oils in a wok or large skillet over a high heat and stirfry the ginger and garlic for 1 minute. Add the zucchini, cabbage and cilantro and stirfry for 3-4 minutes or until the cabbage just begins to wilt.

Remove from the heat, transfer to a large bowl, and stir through the lime juice, zest, peanuts and sesame seeds.

Season with salt and pepper and serve immediately.

SERVES 6.

2 teaspoons sesame oil

2 teaspoons peanut oil

4 cm (1½") piece of fresh ginger, peeled and cut into julienne

1 clove garlic, sliced

2 medium zucchini, thinly sliced

1 small green cabbage, thinly sliced

1 tablespoon fresh cilantro, chopped

grated zest and juice of a lime

1 cup unsalted peanuts, toasted

2 tablespoons sesame seeds, toasted

salt and freshly ground Szechwan pepper

bulgur pilaf

Bulgur wheat originates in the Eastern Mediterranean where it is often soaked in water, squeezed dry and flavored with herbs and spices to serve as a salad. It can also be cooked in a similar way to rice, to produce a light and fluffy pilaf with a delectable nutty flavor.

Preheat the oven to 180°C/350°F.

Bring the stock to the boil. Reduce the heat and hold at a simmer.

Melt the butter in a heavy sauté pan over a medium heat. Add the onion and cook until soft and translucent – about 10 minutes. Reduce the heat to low, add the bulgur and cook, stirring, until the grains are coated with butter.

Add half the hot stock and cook, stirring constantly, until it has been absorbed. Add the remainder of the stock and bring to the boil. Reduce the heat and simmer for about 15 minutes.

Turn the mixture into a baking dish or casserole and bake, uncovered, for 15-20 minutes. Remove from the oven and stir. If the grains are sticky, return to the oven for another 10 minutes or until the grains are dry and separate. Fold through the green onions or herbs, the currants and the nuts.

SERVES 6-8.

3 cups chicken stock (see page 196)

4 tablespoons unsalted butter or olive oil

1 onion, finely chopped (about 1 cup)

$1\frac{1}{2}$ cups bulgur wheat (cracked wheat)
sea salt

1 cup chopped green onions, or fresh mint, parsley or cilantro

$\frac{1}{2}$ cup currants, plumped in hot water and drained

$\frac{1}{2}$ cup toasted almonds or pinenuts

green herb pilaf

This pilaf, which we discovered in Stephanie Alexander's The Cook's Companion, *has became a favorite of Claire Aldous, who has religiously retested every one of the recipes for this book, although she could personally vouch for this one because she'd cooked it so many times! As always, if you use anything but homemade stock, taste before adding salt.*

heat the oil and half the butter in a heavy saucepan. Add the herbs, watercress, green onion and spinach and cook for a few minutes, stirring. Add the rice and cook, stirring until the grains look shiny and are flecked with green. Add the stock and salt. Bring to a boil over a moderate heat, then turn the heat to very low, placing the pan on a simmer mat if you have one. Cover and cook undisturbed for 20 minutes. Stir the remaining butter into the rice with a fork. Turn onto a hot serving dish, grind over pepper and pass the cheese around separately.

SERVES 3-4.

1 tablespoon olive oil

40 g ($2\frac{1}{2}$ tablespoons) unsalted butter

$\frac{1}{2}$ cup parsley, finely chopped

2 tablespoons fresh cilantro, finely chopped

handful watercress leaves, finely chopped

1 cup green onions, finely chopped (including greens)

1 cup packed spinach leaves, washed and stems removed, finely chopped

1 cup long grain rice

$1\frac{1}{2}$ cups chicken stock (see page 196) or water

sea salt and freshly ground black pepper

freshly grated Parmesan or Pecorino cheese

saffron couscous with
spinach and red bell pepper

Couscous is another staple worth keeping in the pantry. North African in origin, this man-made 'grain' is made from semolina and traditionally takes hours of steaming. However, using the instant variety, you can make quick salads or vegetable dishes such as this one, or simply serve it plain with a stew or casserole. Mound it on a plate and pour a hearty soup around it to make a meal go further. What other grain only takes 5 minutes to prepare?

Place the stock and saffron in a pot and simmer for about 10 minutes or until reduced to 2 cups. Set aside.

Melt the butter in a pan over a low heat. Add the pepper and carrot and cook, covered, until tender. Add the green onions and cook until just wilted. Add the couscous, saffron broth and turmeric. Bring to a boil, cover and remove from the heat. Set aside for 5 minutes.

Return the couscous to a low heat, add the garlic and spinach and stir until the spinach is just wilted. Season with salt and pepper and serve at once.

SERVES 4.

$2\frac{1}{2}$ *cups chicken stock (unsalted)*

8-10 saffron threads, toasted carefully in a dry pan

2 tablespoons unsalted butter

$\frac{1}{2}$ *cup red bell pepper, finely diced*

1 carrot, finely julienned

3 green onions, finely chopped

1 cup instant couscous

$\frac{1}{4}$ *teaspoon turmeric*

1 large clove garlic, finely chopped

1 cup tightly packed spinach leaves, washed, dried and coarsely chopped

sea salt and freshly ground black pepper

cakes & cookies

quick almond and plum cake

Sometimes when you need a cake in a hurry, it's hard to find one that is both quick to mix and quick to bake. I tend to go for the quick mix ones, because at least once it's in the oven I can get on and do other things. Use the food processor for this – it takes about 5 minutes.

Preheat the oven to 180°C/350°F. Grease a 24 cm (10") springform cake pan and line the base with baking paper.

In a food processor, combine the flour, almonds, cinnamon and the ⅔ cup of sugar. Process until a coarse powder forms.

Add the eggs, oil, baking powder, vanilla and butter. Process until just incorporated. Add the milk and process until the batter is smooth. Pour the batter into the prepared pan – it should be 2 cm (¾") deep in the pan.

Rinse the whole pitted plums in water and while still wet roll in the remaining sugar. Push the plums down into the cake batter until half submerged.

Place the pan in the center of the oven and bake for 40 minutes or until cake is puffed and brown.

Serve with a dust of icing sugar and lightly whipped cream.

SERVES 8.

1 cup flour

1 cup whole almonds

1 teaspoon cinnamon

⅔ cup plus 3 tablespoons sugar

2 eggs

2 tablespoons canola oil

1 teaspoon baking powder

1 teaspoon vanilla extract

4 tablespoons unsalted butter, softened

⅓ cup milk

6-8 ripe plums, pitted

powdered sugar to dust

apple spiced streusel coffee cake

Apple cakes have been popular for years and almost every family has their favorite. This one has a delicious streusel top and center and looks particularly good baked in a straight-sided ring pan. Look for fresh walnuts that have no hint of bitterness and store them in the freezer to prevent them from going rancid.

Preheat the oven to 180°C/350°F. Butter and flour a 10-cup cake pan.

In a food processor bowl combine the brown sugar, ginger, cinnamon, flour, and butter. Pulse until the mixture resembles large breadcrumbs. Stir in the chopped walnuts. Set aside.

To make the cake, combine the flour, cinnamon, nutmeg, ginger, baking powder, baking soda and salt in a large bowl. In another bowl, use an electric mixer to beat the butter until light and fluffy. Gradually add the sugars and beat until very light. Add the eggs one at a time, beating well after each addition. Gently stir in the apples. Add in half the flour mixture, alternating with the buttermilk, ending with the buttermilk and beating until just mixed.

Spoon half the batter into the prepared pan and sprinkle half the streusel evenly on top. Spoon on the remaining batter, using a rubber spatula to smooth it into an even layer. Sprinkle the remaining streusel evenly over the top and pat it down. Bake for about 1 hour or until a skewer, inserted in the middle, comes out clean. Cool in the pan for 15 minutes before removing. Dust with powdered sugar and serve.

SERVES 8-10.

STREUSEL

$\frac{1}{2}$ cup brown sugar

$\frac{1}{2}$ teaspoon ground ginger

1 teaspoon ground cinnamon

$\frac{1}{2}$ cup flour

60 g (4 tablespoons) cold unsalted
    butter, cut into small pieces

$\frac{1}{2}$ cup walnuts, finely chopped

CAKE

$2\frac{1}{4}$ cups flour

$1\frac{1}{2}$ teaspoons ground cinnamon

$\frac{1}{2}$ teaspoon freshly grated nutmeg

$\frac{1}{2}$ teaspoon ground ginger

1 teaspoon baking powder

1 teaspoon baking soda

$\frac{1}{2}$ teaspoon salt

110 g ($3\frac{1}{2}$ oz) unsalted butter, at room
    temperature

$\frac{3}{4}$ cup packed brown sugar

$\frac{1}{2}$ cup sugar

3 large eggs

2 cooking apples, such as Granny
    Smith or Sturmer, peeled, cored and
    roughly chopped

$1\frac{1}{2}$ cup buttermilk mixed with
    2 teaspoons vanilla extract

powdered sugar

chocolate chunk spice cake

Chocolate goes with many things as you'll discover throughout this book and, yes, in case you're wondering, I do have a passion for chocolate. This cake has a wonderfully light texture, studded with chocolate 'jewels'. It makes a large cake so, as it is better eaten on day one, make sure there are plenty of chocoholics around when you bake it.

Preheat the oven to 180°C/350°F. Grease a 10-cup cake pan or 2 smaller ones with butter and line with baking paper.

Sift the flour with the baking powder, cloves, cinnamon and nutmeg. Set aside.

Cream the butter until soft and gradually add the sugar and continue to cream together until light and fluffy.

Add the eggs one at a time, beating well after each addition. Stir in the chocolate and the mixed peel.

Stir the flour mixture into the butter mixture, alternating with the milk, stirring after each addition until the batter is smooth.

Bake for about 1 hour or until a skewer, inserted in the center, comes out clean. Turn out onto a rack to cool. Dust with powdered sugar and serve with whipped cream.

SERVES AT LEAST 10.

2⅓ cups flour

1½ teaspoons baking powder

¾ teaspoon ground cloves

2 teaspoons cinnamon

½ teaspoon freshly grated nutmeg

120 g (4½ oz) unsalted butter

1½ cups sugar

4 eggs

175 g (1 cup) dark or milk chocolate, grated or in chips

½ cup mixed citrus peel, finely chopped

1 cup milk

powdered sugar to dust

pineapple upside-down cake

You can always gauge how good a cake is by how quickly it disappears. This one disappeared particularly fast when we tested it again for this book!

Although fresh pineapple will give a much more intense flavor to the cake, well drained, canned pineapple can be substituted. Or dispense with pineapple all together and use pears or apples and a little cinnamon or cardamom. This cake also makes a great dessert, served warm with whipped cream.

Preheat the oven to 180°C/350°F. Butter a 24 cm (9½") square or round cake pan and set it on a heat-proof surface.

In a heavy saucepan, combine the water and sugar. Bring to a boil over a medium heat, stirring to dissolve the sugar. Increase the heat and boil steadily, without stirring, until it turns a rich amber color. Remove from the heat and pour into the cake pan. Allow to cool.

Arrange the segments of pineapple on top of the caramel.

With an electric mixer, cream the butter. Gradually add the sugar, beating until the mixture is light. Add the eggs one at a time. Add the vanilla extract.

Sift together the flour, baking powder and salt. Mix half the dry ingredients into the butter mixture, beating just until the flour disappears. Add the buttermilk and mix again. Add the remaining flour, mixing lightly. Spoon large dollops of the batter over the sliced fruit. Smooth out the batter.

Bake the cake for about 45-50 minutes or until it is firm and a deep golden color. Remove from the oven and run a knife between the cake and the tin. Set a serving platter upside down on top of the cake pan and invert the platter and pan. Let rest for 4-5 minutes, to allow the caramel to settle. Gently lift pan from the cake and serve.

SERVES 8.

4 tablespoons water

1 cup sugar

1 large ripe pineapple, peeled and sliced into segments

CAKE

115 g (4 oz) unsalted butter, softened

1 cup sugar

2 eggs

½ teaspoon vanilla extract

1½ cups flour

1 teaspoon baking powder

pinch of salt

½ cup buttermilk

lemon, lime and poppyseed trickle cake

This cake, with its rather fanciful name, is another of the all-time favorite cakes from 'Gourmet on the Run'. The method is fairly standard, but it's the lime and the yogurt that give it a real zing.

Preheat the oven to 180°C/350°F. Grease and flour a 4-cup ring pan.

Place the butter, lime and lemon zests in the large bowl of an electric mixer and beat until light and creamy. Add the sugar gradually and beat well after each addition. Beat in the eggs, one at a time and mix well. Combine the flour, baking powder and poppyseeds and fold in, alternating with the yogurt. Spoon into the prepared pan and bake for 30-35 minutes until a skewer, inserted into the center, comes out clean. Allow to stand in the pan for about 5 minutes, then turn out onto a wire rack.

To make the syrup, place the juices and sugar into a pan. Simmer gently and stir until the sugar dissolves and then bring to a boil, this time without stirring, and boil for 3 minutes.

Set the cake rack over a plate. Make holes all over the top of the cake with a small skewer and pour the hot syrup over the hot cake. Serve warm or cold.

SERVES 8-10.

125 g (4½ oz) unsalted butter, softened

2 teaspoons finely grated lime zest

2 teaspoons finely grated lemon zest

1¼ cups sugar

3 eggs

1½ cups flour

2 teaspoons baking powder

2 tablespoons poppy seeds

100 ml (3½ fl oz) plain yogurt

SYRUP

3 tablespoons lime juice

3 tablespoons lemon juice

3 tablespoons sugar

chocolate hazelnut cake

One of my favorite Australian food writers is Jill Dupleix. I enjoy the many and varied philosophies about food and life found in her books. In New Food *she romanticizes about food and simplifies techniques, and in* Old Food *she delves back in time and brings old dishes back to life. This cake is adapted from one found in* Old Food*. It has links with a traditional flourless chocolate cake, the sort that sinks in the middle and crack on top. It's good!*

Preheat the oven to 180°C/350°F. Butter and flour a 20 cm (8") round cake pan.

Melt the chocolate, coffee, brandy, sugar and butter in a double boiler over simmering water. Remove from the heat and stir until well mixed.

Add the ground nuts and mix well. Beat in the egg yolks one by one. Beat egg whites until stiff and stir a couple of spoonfuls into the chocolate mixture to lighten it, before gently folding in the rest.

Turn into the prepared pan and bake for 40-50 minutes. Leave to cool before removing from pan and don't worry if the crust falls and collapses. That's perfectly normal. Dust with powdered sugar to serve.

SERVES 6-8.

200 g (7 oz) dark chocolate, chopped or in chips

1 tablespoon strong espresso coffee

1 tablespoon brandy

150 g (5½ oz) sugar

150 g (5½ oz) unsalted butter

100 g (⅔ cup) ground hazelnuts

5 eggs, separated

powdered sugar for dusting

yeasted apple tart

Stephanie Alexander's bestselling book The Cook's Companion *has been a source of constant inspiration to everyone who owns a copy, including me. We were delighted to have her as our guest at the Epicurean for the second time in 1996, at the time the book was launched. As I write this in the latter half of 1998 her book is still at the top of the bestseller list of cookbooks. This tart, from* The Cook's Companion, *reminded me of an apple pudding my mother made. It's the sort of thing you could eat for breakfast or with morning coffee.*

Sift the flour, salt and sugar together into a bowl. Sprinkle the yeast over the warm milk and set aside for 5 minutes until the mixture is frothy. Whisk the egg with the yeast and milk and mix into the flour mixture.

Work in the softened butter and knead to a smooth, thick batter. Sprinkle with extra flour, cover and leave to rise in a draft-free place for 30 minutes. Punch down the dough to its original size, then press it into a 22 cm (8½") loose-bottomed tart pan and leave to recover for 30 minutes (it will have puffed slightly).

Meanwhile, preheat the oven to 225°C/450°F.

Peel and core the apples and cut into eighths. Arrange on top of the dough and cover with the brown sugar. Bake for 10 minutes, then reduce the heat to 200°C/400°F. Spoon the cream over the apple and bake for a further 20 minutes. The top should be slightly caramelized and the tart light and spongy. Eat warm.

SERVES 6-8.

250 g (1⅔ cups) flour

pinch of salt

1 tablespoon sugar

1 teaspoon dried yeast

½ cup warm milk

1 egg, beaten

30 g (2 tablespoons) unsalted butter, softened

2 apples

⅓ cup brown sugar

3 tablespoons cream

praline cookies

I first made these lovely cookies with my children, Tom and Olivia, packing them in boxes to give to school teachers and grandparents for Christmas one year. You can make praline and keep it airtight in the freezer. That way it's always on hand to make these cookies, fold through ice-cream or to sprinkle on top of a dessert as a garnish.

butter a baking tray or line with a teflon sheet.

Combine the sugar, water and lemon juice in a small saucepan with a heavy base and stir over a medium heat until the sugar has dissolved. Increase the heat and boil the syrup until it is an even golden brown. Remove from the heat and stir in the nuts. Pour immediately onto the prepared tray and spread to a thin layer.

When cool, pulverize the caramel in a food processor.

Preheat the oven to 170°C/325°F. Butter a baking tray or line with a teflon sheet.

Cream the butter and sugar until light and fluffy. Add the vanilla and salt, then mix in the flour and praline until just combined.

Chill the dough until firm enough to work with. Roll out to 6 mm ($\frac{1}{4}$") thick and cut into shapes.

Place 2$\frac{1}{2}$ cm (1") apart on the tray and bake for 8-10 minutes until golden. Cool and store in an airtight container.

MAKES 4-6 DOZEN SMALL COOKIES.

PRALINE

1 cup sugar

75 ml (2$\frac{1}{2}$ fl oz) water

$\frac{1}{2}$ teaspoon lemon juice

1 cup almonds or pecans

COOKIES

250 g (9 oz) unsalted butter, softened

95 g ($\frac{1}{2}$ cup) brown sugar

$\frac{1}{2}$ teaspoon vanilla extract

$\frac{1}{2}$ teaspoon salt

2 cups flour

$\frac{3}{4}$ cup ground praline

lemon lace cookies

These cookies are from very early in the series but have remained a firm favorite. The recipe came from the famous New Basics Cookbook. *Whenever I suggest serving a crisp cookie with a dessert, these are just what I mean.*

Preheat the oven to 180°C/350°F. Lightly grease two baking trays or line with teflon sheets.

Combine the flour, salt and nuts in a bowl.

Place the brown sugar, corn syrup and butter in a heavy-based saucepan and bring to the boil. Remove from the heat and stir in the flour mixture, along with the lemon zest and juice.

Drop ½ teaspoonfuls of the batter, about 5 cm (2") apart, onto the baking trays. Bake one tray at a time, just until they are lightly browned at the edges – about 8-10 minutes.

Allow to cool slightly before transferring to a rack. Store in an airtight container.

1 cup flour, sifted

¼ teaspoon salt

1 cup finely chopped blanched almonds

¾ cup brown sugar, packed down firmly

½ cup dark corn syrup

110 g (4 oz) unsalted butter

grated zest of 2 lemons

1 tablespoon lemon juice

MAKES ABOUT 50 COOKIES.

pecan nutmeg cake

We really have chosen the very best cakes from our collection to include in this book. This one deserves the title of 'most delicious'. The base turns into crunchy caramel as the cake bakes, making it totally irresistible. It's best eaten fresh.

Preheat the oven to 180°C/350°F. Grease a 20 cm (8") round cake pan with butter and line with baking paper.

Combine the flour, baking powder and sugar in a bowl. Using your fingertips, rub in the butter until the mixture resembles fine breadcrumbs. Sprinkle half the mixture over the base of the cake pan and press down firmly to form a base. Dissolve the soda in the milk and mix in the egg and nutmeg. Add to the remaining flour mixture and combine. Stir in the pecans and pour over the prepared base. Bake for 1 hour or until cooked when tested with a skewer. Leave to cool in the pan. To serve, dust with powdered sugar if desired.

250 g (1⅔ cups) flour, sifted

2 teaspoons baking powder

2 cups lightly packed brown sugar

125 g (4½ oz) unsalted butter, cubed

1 teaspoon baking soda

1 cup milk

1 egg, lightly beaten

1 teaspoon nutmeg, freshly grated

½ cup chopped pecans

SERVES 6-8.

thick & chewy
chocolate chip cookies

Everybody has a favorite chocolate chip cookie recipe. This is ours!

Preheat the oven to 170°C/325°F.

Mix the flour, salt and baking soda together in a medium bowl and set aside.

Either by hand or with an electric mixer, mix the butter and sugars until thoroughly blended. Mix in the egg, yolk and vanilla.

Add the dry ingredients and mix until just combined. Stir in the chocolate.

With a spoon, scoop up $\frac{1}{4}$-$\frac{1}{3}$ cup of dough, form into a rough ball and place on a baking tray lined with a nonstick sheet or baking paper, being careful not to smooth the uneven surface.

Bake until the cookies are light golden brown and the outer edges start to harden yet centers are still soft and puffy —15-18 minutes.

Cool the cookies on baking tray. Store in an airtight container.

MAKES 18 LARGE COOKIES.

2 cups flour

$\frac{1}{2}$ teaspoon salt

$\frac{1}{2}$ teaspoon baking soda

180 g (6$\frac{1}{2}$ oz) unsalted butter, melted and cooled slightly

1 cup brown sugar

$\frac{1}{2}$ cup sugar

1 large egg

1 egg yolk

2 teaspoons vanilla extract

1$\frac{1}{2}$ cups chocolate chips

orange madeleines

These little feathery light tea-cakes are traditionally baked in shell-shaped madeleine molds, which come 12 to a tray. Tiny miniature madeleines are delightful to serve with creamy desserts or as a petit four with coffee. I've tried many different recipes, and this one is by far the best. Create your own flavors – replace the orange with lemon or a teaspoon of vanilla and the spices for others like cinnamon, nutmeg or a mixture. Eat them the day they are baked!

Preheat the oven to 190°C/375°F. Grease and flour a madeleine pan.

Sift the flour, salt, cardamom and almonds together twice. Place the eggs and sugar in a bowl on top of simmering water. Beat with an electric beater until the mixture is thick and creamy. Remove from the heat and continue beating for a further 2-3 minutes.

Combine the melted butter, juice and zest and, using a large metal spoon, carefully fold in alternating with dry ingredients.

Fill each of the madeleine molds three-quarters full and bake for 8-10 minutes until lightly colored.

Cool on a wire rack and dust with powdered sugar before serving.

MAKES 18.

$^3/_4$ cup flour

pinch of salt

$^1/_2$ teaspoon ground cardamom

$^1/_4$ cup ground almonds

2 eggs

$^1/_4$ cup sugar

*150 g (5$^1/_4$ oz) butter, melted and
  cooled*

2 tablespoons orange juice

zest of half an orange, finely grated

powdered sugar for dusting

desserts &
puddings

warm cappuccino bread pudding

We cooked this pudding way back in 1995, but customers still come and tell me they've made it recently and how good it is. Bread and butter puddings have come a long way since the days of sliced white bread, raisins and rather watery custard. I didn't grow up with milk puddings and so my first experience came when I went to live, at age 16, in a nurses' home. The ones I tasted made me thankful my mother didn't cook them. It was much, much later, while cooking in France, that my employer showed me how to make this nursery pudding with day-old croissants, cream instead of milk, and extra egg yolks to enrich it further. Needless to say, I was hooked!

Combine the espresso and 2 tablespoons of sugar in a small saucepan over a medium heat. Stir until the sugar is dissolved. Reduce the mixture to $\frac{1}{2}$ cup and set it aside to cool.

Combine the eggs, yolks and remaining $\frac{1}{3}$ cup sugar in a medium mixing bowl and slowly stir in the cream. Add the cooled espresso mixture and stir until all the ingredients are well mixed.

Preheat the oven to 170°C/325°F.

Layer the croissant slices in a baking dish approximately 23 x 23 x 5 cm (9" x 9" x 2"). Sprinkle the almonds evenly over the croissants. Pour the egg mixture into the dish, making sure that the croissants are submerged. Allow them to absorb all the liquid (about 30 minutes).

Place the baking dish in a roasting pan and pour in 1.25 cm ($\frac{1}{2}$") of boiling water. Bake the pudding for approximately 1 hour until it is golden brown and firm to the touch in the center.

Allow the pudding to sit briefly, before serving hot with softly whipped cream.

SERVES 6-8.

1 cup espresso or strong coffee

2 tablespoons plus $\frac{1}{3}$ cup sugar

3 whole eggs

3 egg yolks

1$\frac{1}{2}$ cups cream

4 cups sliced day-old croissants or brioche

$\frac{1}{2}$ cup sliced almonds, optional

baked peaches stuffed with almonds

This simple summer dessert can be whipped up in seconds. This particular version with crystallized ginger is from Maggie Beer's first book, Maggie's Farm. *Don't worry if your pantry doesn't yield any ginger, as I've made it many times without. Amaretto cookies are a mainstay pantry item. They can be served with coffee at any time of the day, crumbled into ice-cream or sprinkled over fruit salad to jazz it up.*

Preheat the oven to 180°C/350°F.

Halve the peaches and remove the pits. Combine the cookies, almonds and sugar until crumbled. Soften the butter slightly and add it to the crumbs with the ginger to make a paste.

Place the peach halves in a baking dish and mound the mixture into the center of each one. Place $\frac{1}{4}$ cup of dessert wine in the bottom of the dish. Bake in a moderate oven for about 15 minutes, basting with the rest of the wine. Slip off the peach skins if you wish and serve with cream.

SERVES 6.

6 ripe yellow freestone peaches

6 Amaretti cookies

$\frac{3}{4}$ cup whole almonds, toasted

$\frac{1}{2}$ cup (100 g) sugar

200 g (7 oz) unsalted butter

1 teaspoon crystallized ginger, finely chopped

1 cup sweet dessert wine

lemon coconut puddings

These easy little cakes make an elegant dessert. I particularly enjoy them served with homemade lemon curd (see page 193) mixed with whipped cream, with apples poached in a sugar syrup with lemon rind and juice or with a compote of citrus fruits steeped in a sugar syrup (see page 197).

Preheat the oven to 170°C/325°F. Grease 6 x 1 cup molds or large muffin tins.

Cream the softened butter, lemon zest and sugar together until light and creamy. Add the eggs one at a time, beating well after each addition. Fold through the coconut and flour. Spoon the mixture into the prepared molds or muffin tins. Bake for 20 minutes or until golden.

Turn out the cakes onto serving plates and serve hot.

MAKES 6.

125 g (4$\frac{1}{2}$ oz) unsalted butter, softened

3 teaspoons finely grated lemon zest

1 cup sugar

4 eggs

2 cups dried coconut

1 cup self-rising flour

gingerbread with buttered pears and caramel sauce

Ginger and pears just seem to go together. Remember the old upside-down ginger pudding? This rather more modern version consists of three separate components – all simple but exceptional when combined.

Preheat the oven to 180°C/350°F. Grease and flour a savarin mold or a 22 cm (8½") square cake pan.

In a small saucepan, combine the molasses, golden corn syrup, water, butter and brown sugar. Heat slowly, stirring occasionally, until the butter has melted. Stir until well mixed and smooth. Set aside to cool.

In a mixing bowl, combine the remaining dry ingredients. When the molasses mixture has cooled, stir it into the dry ingredients and beat well. Spoon into the prepared pan and bake for 20-25 minutes or until the top springs back when pressed lightly with a fingertip.

Serve warm with the buttered pears, a drizzle of caramel sauce and a little pouring cream.

In a large pan over a medium heat, melt the butter and sprinkle with the sugar. Add half the pears, cut side down and cook until brown – 2-3 minutes. Turn over and repeat. Continue with remaining pears. When cooked, remove with a slotted spoon. Add the brandy to the pan, stirring to mix in any caramelized sugar. Pour over the pears.

In a heavy bottomed saucepan, combine the sugar and water. Cook over a moderate heat, stirring until the sugar is dissolved. Bring the sugar syrup to a boil over a high heat and cook until it turns a rich golden color – about 10 minutes. Take off the heat and carefully add the cream. Place back onto the heat and stir until the mixture is smoothly combined.

SERVES 8.

GINGERBREAD

¼ cup light molasses

¾ cup dark corn syrup

½ cup water

75 g (2¾ oz) unsalted butter

½ cup packed brown sugar

2 cups flour, sifted

2 level tablespoons ground ginger

½ teaspoon cinnamon

¼ teaspoon ground cloves

½ teaspoon salt

1 teaspoon baking soda

BUTTERED PEARS

2 tablespoons unsalted butter

2 tablespoons sugar

4-6 medium pears, peeled, cored and quartered

2 tablespoons brandy

CARAMEL CREAM SAUCE

1 cup sugar

½ cup water

½ cup cream

chocolate pear frangipane tart

Just as ginger and pears are a match, so too are chocolate and pears. The better the chocolate you use in this tart, the better the flavor will be. If you have an abundance of fresh pears, peel and core them and poach gently in a sugar syrup until tender. Cool them in the syrup and use in place of the canned fruit.

Preheat the oven to 150°C/300°F. Break the chocolate into pieces and melt in a bowl over hot water. Cream the butter and sugar until light and fluffy. Beat in the chocolate. Beat the eggs into this mixture, adding a little at a time, alternating with the ground almonds and flour.

Spoon half the frangipane into the tart shell. Arrange the pears on top. Spoon over the rest of the frangipane, smoothing out until level, and sprinkle the top with flaked almonds. Bake for 1 hour or until the filling is firm.

Dust with powdered sugar and serve warm with whipped cream.

SERVES 6.

225 g (8 oz) best quality dark
  chocolate
115 g (4 oz) unsalted butter, softened
115 g (4 oz) sugar
3 eggs, lightly beaten
115 g (4 oz) ground almonds
30 g (6 tablespoons) plain flour
26 cm (10") sweet shortcrust pastry
  shell, baked blind (see page 192)
2 cans of pear halves, well drained
  (10-12 small halves)
1 tablespoon flaked almonds
powdered icing sugar for dusting

marmalade and caramel pudding

Steamed puddings have made a comeback over the last few years, but did they ever really disappear from New Zealand dinner tables? Lighter versions of traditional puddings, like this one from Stephanie Alexander's book Stephanie's Seasons *don't require such long cooking and can be served as a family dessert with cream or as a more elegant dinner party finale with the Orange and Grand Marnier Sauce.*

butter 8 x 125 ml ($4\frac{1}{2}$ fl oz) molds and put 1 spoonful of marmalade in the bottom of each.

Simmer the brown sugar and orange juice together until the sugar is dissolved. Cool the syrup completely.

Cream the butter, zest and egg yolks until fluffy. Pour in the syrup in a thin stream, beating constantly. Add the flour all at once. Mix well. Whisk the egg whites to soft peaks and fold into the mixture.

Fill the prepared molds $\frac{2}{3}$ full. Cover with buttered foil or baking paper and steam the puddings for 20 minutes or until firm.

Turn out and surround with the Orange and Grand Marnier Sauce.

SERVES 8.

6-8 tablespoons marmalade

100 g ($\frac{1}{2}$ cup) brown sugar

$\frac{1}{2}$ cup orange juice

125 g ($4\frac{1}{2}$ oz) unsalted butter

2 tablespoons grated orange zest

3 eggs, separated

150 g (1 cup) self-rising flour

orange and grand marnier sauce

heat the orange juice and Grand Marnier until nearly simmering. Whisk the yolks and sugar until combined. Pour the hot liquid onto the yolk mixture, whisking well.

Return to the pan and cook over a gentle heat, stirring constantly, until thickened. Strain quickly into a bowl set over ice.

200 ml (7 fl oz) strained orange juice

2 tablespoons Grand Marnier

3 egg yolks

80 g ($5\frac{1}{2}$ tablespoons) sugar

caramelized apple clafoutis

A clafoutis is a very traditional French pudding that can be made with any fruit, from berries or grapes to peaches or apricots. In this version the caramelization of the apples and the addition of the Calvados (apple brandy) results in a rich and particularly delicious pudding.

Preheat the oven to 200°C/400°F. Butter a 22 cm (9") baking dish.

In a bowl, toss the apples with the lemon juice and the Calvados.

In a mixer, beat the eggs with $\frac{1}{3}$ cup of sugar for 1-2 minutes until the mixture lightens and doubles in volume. Stir in the flour, cream, vanilla and the Calvados; whisk until smooth. Pour $1\frac{1}{2}$ cups of the batter into the baking dish and bake for 5-6 minutes on the lower rack until it is just beginning to set but not yet browned.

Meanwhile caramelize the apples. Put the butter and sugar in a frying pan. Cook over a high heat, stirring to prevent the sugar from burning, until it caramelizes – approximately 2 minutes. Add the apples to the pan, reserving the lemon juice and Calvados. Swirl the pan to stop the sugar from browning. Cook the apples over a high heat, stirring as necessary to prevent sticking. Continue until the apples are clinging to one another and the juices are richly colored – approximately 8-10 minutes. Remove the pan from the heat and add the reserved lemon juice and Calvados, covering briefly to trap the vapors. Transfer the apples to the baking dish and spread them out evenly on top of the partially cooked batter.

Raise the oven temperature to 240°C/475°F. Whisk the melted, cooled butter gradually into the remaining batter and pour this mixture over the apples. Bake for another 12-15 minutes until the top is set and lightly browned all over.

Remove from the oven and allow to cool for 10-15 minutes. Serve with whipped cream.

SERVES 6-8.

APPLES

600 g (1 lb 5 oz) tart apples, peeled, cored and each cut into 8-12 slices

1 tablespoon lemon juice

2 tablespoons Calvados or brandy

$\frac{1}{4}$ cup unsalted butter

$\frac{2}{3}$ cup sugar

BATTER

2 eggs, lightly beaten

$\frac{1}{3}$ cup sugar

6 tablespoons flour

$\frac{3}{4}$ cup cream

1 teaspoon vanilla extract

1 tablespoon Calvados

$\frac{1}{4}$ cup unsalted butter, melted but not hot

whipped cream for serving

white chocolate mousse
with frangelico

White chocolate flavored with hazelnut liqueur is fairly irresistible. Other combinations work well too – try orange, coffee or mint liqueurs and serve this mousse with a crisp cookie.

Melt the white chocolate and butter in a double boiler. Set aside.

In a large, heat-proof bowl, beat the egg yolks, sugar and liqueur until the mixture forms a slowly dissolving ribbon when the beaters are lifted. Place the bowl over a saucepan half-filled with simmering water and cook, whisking constantly, until very thick – about 5 minutes. Remove from the heat.

Whisk in the white chocolate mixture and stir until smooth and cool.

Beat the cream until peaks are stiff. In a separate bowl with clean beaters, beat the egg whites with the cream of tartar until stiff but not dry. Gently fold the egg whites into the chocolate mixture, then fold in the whipped cream.

Spoon the mousse into individual dishes (approximately 175 ml/ 6 fl oz). Refrigerate covered until set – about 3 hours. Sprinkle with Dutch cocoa powder just before serving.

SERVES 10-12.

225 g (8 oz) white chocolate, broken into small pieces

110 g (4 oz) unsalted butter

6 eggs, separated, at room temperature

1 cup sifted powdered sugar

$\frac{1}{2}$ cup Frangelico liqueur

500 ml (17$\frac{1}{2}$ fl oz) cream, cold

pinch of cream of tartar

unsweetened Dutch cocoa powder to garnish

treacle tart

This tart can be made using both a top and bottom crust or with a decorative lattice top. Sometimes I use different shapes – stars and moons, hearts or leaves, for added interest. When using unbaked tart bases, it's a good idea to give an extra burst of heat to the base – simply place a baking sheet in the oven as it preheats and slide the tart onto this.

Preheat the oven to 220°C/450°F.

Line a 24 cm (10") tart pan, with a removable base, with half the pastry. Chill. Warm the corn syrup and add all ingredients for the filling. Pour into the pastry case.

Smooth the top and use the remaining pastry to cover completely or make a lattice top. Seal the edges very well and crimp them if you wish. Alternatively, lay pastry cutouts on the top.

Bake for 30 minutes or until the pastry is golden and crisp. Remove the tart, brush the top crust with the egg white and sprinkle with sugar. Return the tart to the oven for a further 5 minutes to glaze the top.

SERVES 8.

250 g (9 oz) sweet short pastry (see page 195)
1 egg white
sugar

FILLING

2 cups dark corn syrup
3 cups fresh white breadcrumbs
juice and grated zest of a large lemon
a few pieces of candied orange zest, finely chopped

182

upside-down pear and raisin tart

This ultra-simple tart is one that tops the list of all-time favorites. It's a variation on the famous French tarte tatin that everyone loves. Make sure you use big, fat raisins that plump up beautifully when steeped in the wine.

Preheat the oven to 200°C/400°F.

Put the raisins in a small saucepan and pour over all but 2 tablespoons of the wine. Cover and heat until just bubbling, stir, cover again and set aside until the raisins have absorbed the wine.

Meanwhile put the butter, sugar and the remaining wine in a 25 cm (10") ovenproof, cast-iron frying pan. Cook, stirring constantly, until the mixture is a golden brown caramel. Cool.

Halve, peel and core the pears. Make a ring of them in the prepared pan, rounded sides down, tips pointing to the center. Fill their centers with some of the raisins and distribute the rest among the pear halves.

Lay the chilled pastry over the pears and tuck the edge down inside the pan. Cut several slits in the top.

Bake for about 30 minutes or until the pears are tender and the pastry is golden brown and cooked.

Set a serving plate upside down on top of the pan and, holding the two together tightly, flip over. Serve immediately with cream.

SERVES 6-8.

$\frac{3}{4}$ cup lexia or muscatel raisins

$\frac{1}{2}$ cup sweet dessert wine

2 tablespoons unsalted butter

2 tablespoons sugar

1 kg (2 lb) Bosc or Winter Nelis pears – or enough to cover the bottom of the pan with halved pears

1 x 25 cm (10") square of puff pastry

lightly whipped cream, for topping

nectarine and raspberry crostata

Freeform tarts are particularly quick and easy. This combination of nectarines and raspberries is a favorite, but also try it with apples tossed in brown sugar and spices, pears and lexia raisins, or peaches and blueberries.

Mix the flour, sugar and salt in a food processor. Add the butter, pulsing until the mixture resembles coarse breadcrumbs. Add the water by tablespoonfuls and process just until moist clumps form. Gather the dough into a ball, flatten into a disc and chill at least 1 hour. This can be made a day ahead. Keep well chilled and soften slightly before rolling.

Place a baking tray in the oven and preheat the oven to 190°C/375°F.

Roll out the dough on lightly floured baking paper, or a teflon sheet, to 6 mm (¼") thick round. Trim the dough to a 35 cm (14") round. Transfer the dough on its paper to a second large baking tray. Mash ½ cup of raspberries in a large bowl. Add the sliced nectarines, sugar and lemon juice and toss to coat. Gently add the remaining raspberries. Spoon into the center of the dough, leaving a 7½ cm (3") border. Sprinkle the fruit with 2 tablespoons of sugar. Fold the border over the fruit, pinching to fit and to seal any cracks. Brush the dough with beaten egg and sprinkle with a little sugar. If the dough has softened, chill again until firm.

Place the tray directly onto the preheated baking sheet. Bake the crostata until the pastry is golden and the filling bubbles – about 35 minutes. Cool slightly before serving with whipped cream.

SERVES 8.

PASTRY

2 cups plain flour

¼ cup sugar

½ teaspoon salt

240 g (8¼ oz) unsalted butter, chilled and chopped

2 tablespoons ice-cold water

FILLING

1½ cups fresh raspberries

4-5 ripe nectarines, pitted and sliced

⅓ cup sugar plus 2 tablespoons extra

1 teaspoon lemon juice

1 egg, beaten lightly

lightly whipped cream, for topping

These days, with the availability of moderately priced electric ice-cream machines, it's easy enough to whip up your own iced treats using only fresh ingredients. There are, however, many frozen desserts that need no churning, among them semifreddos and granitas.

lemon nougat semifreddo

The Italians are famous for their semifreddo or soft ice-creams. They are so much easier to make than traditional ice-cream. This one and the lemon semifreddo that follows are both good to make ahead, as they store well in the freezer for at least a week. After that the flavor tends to deteriorate.

Process the ricotta and sugar in a food processor until smooth.

Finely chop the nougat or wrap in a tea-towel and smash with a rolling pin until broken into small pieces.

Whip the cream until soft peaks form. Combine the ricotta mixture, nougat, cream and zests in a bowl and mix well. Pour into a 2-liter mold that has been rinsed in cold water. Freeze until set. Turn out onto a platter and serve cut into slices with lime slices or fresh seasonal fruits.

SERVES 10-12.

700 g (1lb 9 oz) ricotta

300 g (10½ oz) sugar

300 g (10½ oz) brittle nougat with almonds (purchased)

500 ml (2 cups) cream

finely grated zest of half a lemon

finely grated zest of 1 lime

lemon semifreddo

Serve this refreshing iced dessert with fresh raspberries or simply a crisp little cookie such as the Lemon Lace Cookies on page 168.

Line a 6-cup mold with doubled tinfoil or baking paper.

Beat the egg yolks and vanilla with an electric beater until thick and lemon colored.

Put the sugar, milk and lemon zest in a heavy-based saucepan and heat gently, stirring until the sugar is dissolved. When it reaches scalding point, add the lemon juice and pour onto the yolks, whisking constantly. Beat well and allow to cool.

Whip the cream and fold in with a large spoon.

Pour half the mixture into the prepared mold. Add the finely chopped glacé peel into the other half and pour on top.

Freeze until firm, turn out onto a platter and slice.

SERVES 8.

4 egg yolks

2 drops vanilla extract

¾ cup (175 g) sugar

60 ml (4 tablespoons) milk

finely grated zest of 1 lemon

80 ml (5 tablespoons) lemon juice

500 ml (2 cups) cream

1 tablespoon candied peel, finely chopped

Lemon Nougat Semifreddo (left)

coffee granita

This is a fun thing to serve on a hot summer's day, and the only piece of equipment you need is a fork (and a freezer of course)! What other dessert can you think of that only has two ingredients and yet tastes so good. The Dutch cocoa referred to here is cocoa powder that has an added alkaline agent that takes away the bitter taste and gives it a lovely dark color.

Combine the hot coffee and sugar and stir until the sugar dissolves. Set aside to cool. Pour into a shallow cake tin or freezer-proof container, cover and freeze until the mixture is partially set. Stir with a fork and return to the freezer until completely set. Using a fork, break up the granita into small crystals and return to the freezer for 1 hour before serving.

Serve plain or layered with whipped cream in tall glasses or espresso cups, topped with a spoonful of whipped cream and dusted with Dutch cocoa.

3 cups freshly made strong black espresso coffee

½ cup sugar

whipped cream and Dutch cocoa to serve

SERVES 6-8.

strawberry gelato

The action of churning ice-cream as it freezes inhibits the formation of ice crystals, resulting in a smooth, creamy texture. The higher the fat content, the less necessary churning becomes. Gelato, with its high water content, does need churning. It's worth it though, because homemade gelato is nothing like the commercial equivalent.

Wash the berries in cold water, then hull and cut in half.

Put the strawberries and sugar in the bowl of a food processor and pulse. Add the water and blend until puréed.

Whip the cream until it thickens slightly to the consistency of buttermilk. Combine thoroughly with the puréed strawberries.

Pour into an ice-cream machine and freeze.

250 g (8 oz) fresh strawberries

¾ cup sugar

¾ cup cold water

¼ cup cold cream

SERVES 4-6.

strawberry tortoni

This is such a versatile dessert. Use different shaped molds to suit the occasion – a loaf pan for easy slicing, a ring pan so you can fill the center with fresh berries, individual molds for an elegant dinner party. Vary the berries too, changing the liqueur to suit. If you use frozen berries be sure to thaw and drain them thoroughly before use.

Line a 10-cup mold with tinfoil.

Mix the strawberries, almonds, Amaretti and the liqueur together in a bowl. Stand for 10 minutes to allow the flavors to infuse.

Whip the egg whites until stiff, but not dry. Add the powdered sugar and a pinch of cream of tartar and beat until shiny.

Whip the cream and combine with the fruit. Fold in the meringue, lightly but thoroughly.

Pour into the prepared mold and freeze.

When the tortoni is frozen, turn out of the mold onto a plate.

Crush the berries with a fork, sweeten to taste with a little sugar and fold through the whipped cream.

Spread the fool over the top and sides of the ice-cream and refreeze until set.

Remove from the freezer a few minutes before serving to allow the tortoni to soften slightly. Garnish with fresh berries.

SERVES 10.

1 cup roughly chopped strawberries

$\frac{1}{2}$ cup toasted flaked almonds

6 Amaretto cookies, crushed

4 tablespoons brandy or strawberry liqueur

2 egg whites

$\frac{1}{2}$ cup powdered sugar

pinch cream of tartar

500 ml (2 cups) cream

FOOL

1 basket of ripe strawberries

sugar to taste

300 ml (10$\frac{1}{2}$ fl oz) cream, whipped

lemon soufflé with lemon curd

Use the intensely aromatic Meyer lemons for these soufflés, as they are sweeter and have a lower acidity than other varieties. Juice them only when needed, as lemon juice tends to deteriorate rapidly. When you order a soufflé in a restaurant, chances are it will have been made a few hours ahead, refrigerated and then baked to order. The secret is in the meringue, which holds well without separating. Try this one at your next dinner party. Prepare them in the afternoon and have them in the fridge ready to bake.

Place the 100 ml of lemon juice and the zest in a small saucepan and cook gently until it forms a paste.

Preheat the oven to 190°C/375°F. Butter 8 x 1-cup molds and coat the buttered surface with sugar, tapping out any excess.

Place the yolks, lemon juice and the cooked zest in a bowl over simmering water. Whisk until it has a creamy, frothy consistency.

Whisk the egg whites until stiff, gradually adding the sugar to make a meringue. Fold the two mixtures together and spoon into the prepared molds. Run a knife around the edge – this helps the soufflés to rise. Bake for 10 minutes until puffed and golden, but still creamy in the center.

Serve immediately with lemon curd (see page 193) and cream.

SERVES 8.

100 ml ($3\frac{1}{2}$ fl oz) lemon juice

zest of 4-5 lemons

10 eggs, separated

180 ml ($6\frac{1}{2}$ fl oz) lemon juice, strained

400 g ($1\frac{3}{4}$ cups) sugar

lemon curd and clotted cream to serve

glossary

Arborio rice see risotto.

baking blind This term refers to the baking of an unfilled pastry case. Once the pastry has been rolled out and fitted into the pan, line it with a sheet of baking paper, fitting it into the edges of the tart. To prevent the pastry from collapsing during baking, fill with ceramic or metal baking beans and place in a hot, 200°C/400°F, oven to bake. After about 20 minutes remove the beans and paper and return to the oven until the pastry is cooked.

balsamic vinegar A good balsamic vinegar is 'sweet' and viscous, and makes a superb vinaigrette when combined with olive oil. Use it to heighten the flavor of hearty casseroles, sauces or marinades. Since its popularization, the quality of balsamic vinegar has dropped. Cheap balsamics are usually nothing more than red wine vinegar with caramel added.

buttermilk Once the residue left from butter making, buttermilk is now a cultured skim milk. It is thick and slightly acid and can be used in drinks and cake baking.

chocolate Since the days when cocoa beans were used as currency by the Mayans, chocolate has been revered. Today the quality of chocolate varies considerably – cheap cooking chocolate will do nothing to enhance the flavour of a cake or dessert. Use the best chocolate you can find – this means a product very high (more than 55%) in cocoa butter. Look for the brands Valhrona or Callebaut.

Chocolate burns easily so follow these steps:

- Chop the chocolate up into small bits so it will melt evenly.
- Place it in a bowl over simmering water to ensure a gentle heat.
- Stir constantly until smooth.
- Prevent the introduction of water or steam – this will cause the chocolate to solidify (seize).
- If using a microwave, use short bursts of heat and stir the chocolate between each one.

chiles Many of the dishes in this book call for fresh or dried chiles or dried chile flakes. I make my own chile flakes by crushing dried red chiles. Chiles vary in their heat – a general rule of thumb is the smaller the chile, the hotter it will be. The only real way to find out though is to have a taste!

chorizo A spicy Spanish sausage containing pork, spices and chile.

couscous A form of pasta used in North African cuisine – coarsely ground semolina is mixed to a dough with water and salt and rolled into tiny balls that are steamed. Today the 'instant' variety is widely used.

crostini Slices of French bread, brushed with olive oil and baked in the oven until crisp and golden. Store in an airtight container.

Dutch cocoa The process of dutching refers to the addition of an alkaline to cocoa, which gives it a dark color and removes any bitter taste.

fenugreek The seed of the fenugreek plant belonging to the pea family. It is either soaked overnight until it swells and then used in cooking, or it is roasted briefly, ground and used like a spice.

fish sauce *(nuoc ma'm or nam pla)* I call it the salt of South East Asia. It is a clear, amber liquid derived from fermented fish. Used as a flavoring and in dipping sauces. Keeps indefinitely. It tastes much better than it smells.

flat-leaf parsley An essential pantry item – also called Italian or continental parsley, it has a much better flavor and texture than the commonly-known curly parsley.

- easy to grow in pots or the garden for a constant supply.
- reserve the stems and freeze for use in stocks.
- store in the fridge with the stems in a little water and a plastic bag over the leaves.
- chop with a large cook's knife, rather than a food processor which tears the leaves.

lemon curd This old-fashioned curd keeps well for several weeks in the fridge. Spread it on fresh bread or serve it on ice-cream or with puddings.

> *225 g (8oz) unsalted butter*
> *350 g (12 oz) sugar*
> *zest of 6 lemons, finely grated*
> *300 ml (11 fl oz) lemon juice, strained*
> *6 large eggs, beaten and strained*

Melt the butter and add the sugar, lemon zest and juice. Stir to dissolve the sugar and remove from the heat. Add the eggs, beating well with a wooden spoon. Return to a medium heat and stir until thick – do not allow to boil.

Cool and store covered in the fridge.

lemongrass A fibrous grass, valued for its flavor. Use only the bulbous root end and the core.

lemons About 4000 years ago the lemon began its journey from India through China and on to North Africa and the Mediterranean, from where it was taken to the New World. Nowadays, no pantry is complete without a constant supply of lemons. Besides fresh, they come pickled, dried, preserved and candied. The two we see most are sweet and juicy Meyer lemons with their lovely thin, bright yellow skins and Lisbons, which have pale knobbly skins, are deliciously sour and difficult to juice.

Use them to:
- stop apples, pears or artichokes from going brown.
- balance a rich sauce such as hollandaise or mayonnaise.
- set jams and jellies.
- pep up marinades, soups, fish and sauces.
- ward off colds.
  And:
- to make juicing lemons easy, heat the fruit in the microwave for a few seconds, or place on a firm surface and roll vigorously under your palm.
- store at room temperature for a week or up to a month in the fridge.
- remove the zest first and then juice.
- invest in a zester.
- lemon juice and zest freeze well in ice cube trays.
- to ensure a year-round supply of lemons on your tree, thin the crop by about half.

lentilles de Puy A particularly fine green lentil produced organically in France. They require no soaking and cook in about 25 minutes. Available at delicatessens.

mascarpone A rich, fresh cow's milk cheese of Italian origin. Somewhat like a very soft cream cheese it is most often used in baking and desserts.

mirin A type of rice wine or 'sweet sake' with added sugar, used in cooking.

nori Paper-thin sheets of seaweed used in sushi-making.

olive oil You'll see that most, if not all, the recipes call for extra virgin olive oil. I generally have two oils in my pantry: one estate-bottled, which is used when oil will be a predominant flavor, i.e., drizzled over tomatoes. The other is a moderately priced extra virgin olive oil, which I cook with, use in pasta sauces and in everyday vinaigrettes.

Keep your olive oil in a cool, dark pantry and use within six to eight weeks of opening, so don't buy huge quantities at once. You can decant a little at a time into an oil can to have on hand by the stove. The life of olive oil is about 1 year from bottling.

orzo A small rice-shaped pasta, used in soups, salads or pilaf style dishes.

pancetta Italian bacon that comes tightly rolled. Unsmoked, it has a milder flavor than bacon. Before slicing paper-thin, the rind should be removed.

Parmesan cheese Throughout this book when I refer to Parmesan I do not mean the canisters of granules of the same name. I urge you to look for Italian Parmagiano Reggiano, the finest of Parmesan cheeses from the Italian region of Parma, and buy a small wedge, with the rind on. Store it, wrapped in muslin, in a plastic container with a lid, in the fridge. Grate or shave the cheese as you need it or serve it with fresh pears instead of dessert. Stored correctly, it will last for months. A good alternative is *grana padano*, a similar cheese made in other regions of Italy.

pasta Fresh and dried are not better or worse than each other, just different. A box of best quality dried pasta is far better than a mediocre fresh pasta or vice versa. Making your own pasta provides pleasure and the satisfaction of making something with your own hands that others will enjoy.

- Cook pasta, fresh or dried in abundant boiling water with salt.
- The water should be kept at a rolling boil throughout the cooking.
- Stir the pasta often – there is no need to add oil to the water.
- Taste for doneness – there should be a slight firmness to the bite (al dente). Fresh pasta may take only 2-3 minutes. Dried can take up to 12 minutes.
- Drain immediately and toss with the sauce. A little of the cooking water can be used to lighten the sauce.
- The sauce should cling to the pasta, not pool in the bottom of the bowl.
- Heat the serving bowl, as pasta cools down quickly.

basic egg pasta It is sometimes possible to buy imported Italian pasta flour made from durum wheat. I have always substituted a mixture of high grade (strong) flour and semolina flour (see 'flour' page 193). This seems to give a similar texture and color to the pasta.

1 cup high grade flour
1 cup semolina flour
3 eggs
$\frac{1}{2}$ teaspoon salt
1 tablespoon olive oil

Sift the flours onto the counter in a mound and make a large well in the center. Put the eggs, salt and oil in the well. Mix the liquid ingredients together with a fork and then gradually start to incorporate the flour until the dough becomes like a thick batter. Continue mixing the flour and dough together with your hands to form a ball. Scrape up any remaining flour and sift to remove lumps. Use this flour during the rolling of the dough.

Knead the dough until it is smooth and starting to feel elastic – about 2-3 minutes. The rest of the kneading will be done by the machine. Divide the dough in two. Wrap one half in plastic wrap. Flatten the other half into a rectangle and dust well with flour.

Set the rollers on the pasta machine to the widest setting and pass the dough through. Fold the dough in three and press together firmly to remove any air. Pass through the widest setting again. Repeat this process 8-10 times until the dough is smooth and elastic.

The dough is now ready to be stretched. Pass the dough through the rollers, each time moving the rollers until you have reached the narrowest setting. Do not fold the dough again. Flour the dough between each successive rolling. Pull the pasta to its full length and cut or use as desired.

pastry Most pastries can be made successfully in a food processor as long as care is taken not to over-mix. Uncooked pastry freezes well.

rich shortcrust pastry
170 g (6 oz) plain flour
pinch salt
100 g ($3\frac{1}{2}$ oz) unsalted butter
1 egg yolk
1 tablespoon ice-cold water

In the bowl of the food processor combine the flour, salt and butter. Process briefly until the mixture resembles breadcrumbs. Mix the egg yolk and water together and, using the pulse button, add to the dry ingredients through the feed tube. Mix only until the mixture is just combined. Tip out onto the counter and bring together quickly with your hands. Form into a flat disc, wrap in plastic film and refrigerate for 20-30 minutes before rolling.

pate sucrée – sweet short pastry

170 g (6 oz) plain flour
pinch of salt
85 g (3 oz) sugar
85 g (3 oz) unsalted butter, diced and chilled
3 egg yolks, lightly beaten
2 drops vanilla extract

Place the flour, salt and sugar in the bowl of a food processor and pulse briefly. Drop in the butter and process until the mixture resembles breadcrumbs.
Using the pulse button, pour in the egg yolks and vanilla and blend until just combined. Tip the mixture out onto the counter and bring together quickly by hand. Form into a flat disc, wrap in plastic film and refrigerate for at least 30 minutes before rolling.

Pecorino cheese A cooked hard cheese from Sardinia or Rome, made from sheep's milk. Although used in a similar way, it is sharper in flavor than Parmesan.

polenta A grainy flour made from yellow or white corn. Can be cooked like a porridge or allowed to set so it can be sliced and grilled. The Italians use only water or a little milk when cooking polenta, but I find it has more flavor when cooked in a light chicken or vegetable stock.

porcini The Italian name for cèpes. These tasty mushrooms are available only in their dried form. To soften, cover with boiling water for 30 minutes. Drain and reserve the soaking liquid for use in a soup or sauce.

prosciutto Italian ham or Parma ham – made using the hind legs of specially raised pigs. It is dry-cured in salt and spices and air-dried. Ask to have the rind removed before slicing and ensure the slices are paper thin and kept separate from one another.

punch down A term used in breadmaking that refers to gently pushing out the air that is trapped in the risen dough, returning the dough to its original size before shaping or a second rise.

roasted pepper Red, green, yellow, orange and black – peppers come in myriad colors, but taste much the same. Roasting or grilling sweetens the flesh and removes the thin, bitter skin. It can also add a delicious barbecue flavor.
- To roast: place the peppers on a baking tray in a hot 200°C/400°F oven and roast until the skin is black and blistered. Remove and cover with tinfoil or a clean teatowel. When cool enough to handle, peel off the skin.
- To grill or barbecue: Hold the pepper over the flame of a gas burner or place on the open grill of a barbecue. When the skin is charred and blistered, remove and follow the steps described above.
- Resist the temptation to peel the pepper under running water. This will wash away all the flavor. Simply wash your hands as you peel.

rice noodles different varieties exist: fresh or dried.
rice stick noodles – soak for 30 seconds in cold water, boil for 4-7 minutes.
rice vermicelli – deep-fry in hot oil to make nests or soak for 2 minutes in boiling water before using.
fresh rice noodles – rinse in warm water and add to stirfries or soups.

rice paper Sheets of brittle rice 'paper' are made from a paste of rice flour, water and salt, pressed and dried. To soften, soak each one in warm water. Not to be confused with the European rice paper, which is used under panforte and nougat.

rice vinegar A Chinese vinegar that can be red, black or white. The white is most commonly used as a flavoring agent in soups and in sweet and sour dishes.

shallot A small, mild copper colored onion with pink flesh, commonly used for delicate sauces or for adding raw to dishes. Several varieties are now grown.

shrimp paste A pungent paste of fermented shrimp used to flavor dishes. Keeps indefinitely. Seal it well!

stocks Stock is the most important liquid base used in the preparation of many dishes, such as soups, sauces, casseroles, etc. These days it is possible to buy commercial stocks. Most have added salt so it is advisable to dilute them well before use.

Good, natural stocks are inexpensive to prepare, and if made correctly will greatly enhance the finished dish.

beef stock

> $1\frac{1}{2}$ kg ($3\frac{1}{2}$ lb) beef bones
> 5 liters ($8\frac{3}{4}$ pints) cold water
> 100 g (4 oz) each carrot, onion, celery and leeks
> 1 bouquet garni – a bayleaf, parsley stalks and sprig of thyme
> about 12 peppercorns
> OPTIONAL
> 100 g (4 oz) tomatoes
> $\frac{3}{4}$ oz) mushroom trimmings

- Have the bones chopped small. Remove any fat.
- Place the bones in a roasting dish and roast at 200°C/ 400°F until the bones have become an even brown color.
- Drain off fat and place the bones in a large stockpot.
- Cover with the cold water and bring to a boil. Skim well.
- Wash, trim and cut the carrots, onions, leeks and celery roughly.
- Fry vegetables in a little hot oil or butter until golden brown.
- Drain and add vegetables, bouquet garni and peppercorns to the stock pot.
- Simmer gently for approximately 6 hours, skimming where necessary.
- Strain, cool rapidly and store in the refrigerator until required.
- To reduce to a glace, remove any solidified fat. Bring to the boil and simmer gently until the stock has reduced by three-quarters. Cool, pour into ice cube trays and freeze. Each cube will reconstitute to approximately 1 cup of stock.

chicken stock This is a general purpose stock that is used in recipes where a compatible flavor and color is not essential.

> $1\frac{1}{2}$ kg ($3\frac{1}{2}$ lb) chicken bones
> 5 liters ($8\frac{3}{4}$ pints) cold water
> 100 g (4 oz) each carrot, onion, celery and leeks
> 1 bouquet garni – a bayleaf, parsley stalks and sprig of thyme
> about 12 peppercorns

- Have the bones chopped small. Remove any fat.
- Place the bones in a stock pot, cover with water, bring to a boil and skim well.
- (You can strain this water off instead of skimming and replenish with the fresh water.)
- Peel the carrots and onions. Wash and drain the celery and leeks.
- Add the vegetables, bouquet garni and peppercorns to the stock pot.
- Simmer gently for approximately 6 hours, skimming where necessary.
- Strain, cool rapidly and keep in the refrigerator for further use.

fish stock Cook fish stock for only 20 minutes. After that the bones will start to break down and impart a bitter flavor.

> 1 onion
> 30 g (1 oz) butter
> $\frac{1}{2}$ bayleaf
> 4-6 peppercorns
> few stalks parsley
> juice of 1 lemon
> 1 kg (2 lb) fresh fish bones (well washed)
> $2\frac{1}{2}$ liters ($4\frac{1}{2}$ pints) cold water

- Slice the onion.
- Heat the butter in a deep saucepan and add the onion, bayleaf, peppercorns, parsley, lemon juice and fish bones.
- Cover and stew lightly for 5 minutes, without browning.
- Add the cold water and bring to a boil, skim and simmer gently for 20 minutes.
- Strain immediately and refrigerate.

sugar syrup Using equal quantities of sugar and water, dissolve the sugar in the water over a gentle heat. Increase the heat and boil for 5 minutes. Cool and refrigerate for up to six months.

verjuice In the 14th and 15th centuries French cooks used this juice made from unripe grapes. It has the tartness of lemon and the acidity of vinegar but without the harshness of either. Use it to deglaze pans, make vinaigrettes, or poach fruit in a syrup made from equal parts verjuice and sugar. Read Maggie Beer's books for many ideas. Maggie makes it, the Epicurean imports it.

Vietnamese mint This herb is not a member of the mint family and has a spicy, citrus flavor. It can be recognized by its long, pointed, red tinged leaf. Available in Asian markets.

wasabi A pale green paste made from the very hot root of a native Japanese plant. Available ready made in a tube or as a powder, which is then mixed with water.

wonton wrappers Small squares of pastry used for wontons or spring rolls. Available fresh or frozen they also come in various sizes and thicknesses. Can be used instead of pasta for ravioli.

yeast Allow 7.5 g or $1\frac{1}{2}$ teaspoons dried yeast per 500 g flour.

1 packet dried yeast = 15 g or 1 tablespoon

$1\frac{1}{2}$ teaspoons dried yeast = 1 tablespoon compressed yeast

7.5 g dried yeast = 15 g compressed yeast

STANDARD MEASUREMENTS

Always follow one set of measures in a recipe. Do not mix them up.

Teaspoon, tablespoon and cup measures are level, not heaped, unless otherwise indicated.

The measurements in this book are based on the following and in some cases have been rounded to the nearest ounce in the conversion from metric.

1 teaspoon	= 5 ml
1 tablespoon	= 15 ml/$\frac{1}{2}$ fl oz (Australia = 20 ml)
1 oz/fl oz	= 28.35 g/ml

1 UK pint	= 20 fl oz/567 ml
1 US pint	= 16 fl oz
1 liter	= 35 fl oz (1 US quart)

Wherever possible, measurements have been given in cups rather than weight. However, sometimes weight remains the most accurate measure and cannot be converted exactly to a cup measure.

eggs Unless large eggs are specified, size 6 eggs have been used. This is a standard size egg.

Large eggs are size 7.

index

saffron: Kashmiri lamb koftas in saffron sauce 121
saffron couscous with spinach and red
bell pepper 155
salads: Chinese noodle salad with citrus and spicy
peanuts 137
eggplant with pomegranate sauce 131
grilled niçoise salad 107
herbed orzo with asparagus, chickpeas and feta
dressing 129
Jersey Bennes with bacon and cayenne-toasted
pecans 134
lamb, eggplant and orzo salad 117
parsley and grilled vegetable salad 135
Tuscan salad 138
Vietnamese minted lemon beef salad 130
warm potato and mussel salad 140
warm prawn and scallop salad with arugula 89
wilted spinach salad with roasted bell
pepper 132
salsa agresto 14
saucy chicken and arugula meatballs 126
sausage: orzo risotto with mussels and spicy
sausage 71
scallops: mini chicken and scallop fritters 23
shellfish risotto 74
warm prawn and scallop salad with arugula 89
seaweed: tuna in seaweed with pickled ginger
sauce 109
sesame oil: stir-fried sesame cabbage with
ginger 152
shellfish risotto 74
snapper: baby snapper on Thai curry
vegetables 102
soups: butternut, carrot and cilantro soup 47
Chinese chicken soup 42
cream of roasted vegetable soup 46
laksa 43
potato-tomato soup with rosemary 51
spring vegetable soup 41
Vietnamese beef soup 44
South Indian spicy lentil stew 94
spaghetti with arugula, tomato and avocado 62
spicy gazpacho sauce 23
spinach: chicken and spinach phyllo pie 124
Greek omelette with spinach, feta and dill 53
saffron couscous with spinach and red bell
pepper 155
spinach and blue cheese tarts 80
spinach and feta eccles 11
wilted spinach salad with roasted bell
pepper 132
spring rolls 25
spring vegetable soup 41
stir-fried chile pork with cashews 116
stir-fried sesame cabbage with ginger 152
strawberry gelato 188
strawberry tortoni 189
stuffed pasta with feta, tomatoes and mint 60

tarte tatin provençal 85
tarts *see* **pies and tarts**
ten-minute stroganoff 115
thick & chewy chocolate chip cookies 169
thyme: rabbit with mushrooms and thyme 122
tomatoes: couscous and vegetable stew 87
gratin of eggplant with tomato and basil
vinaigrette 144
lamb with orzo and a spiced tomato sauce 111
lasagne with tomato cream sauce 59
paillard of beef with watercress,

olives and tomatoes 118
parsley and grilled vegetable salad 135
pissaladière 77
polenta with grilled summer vegetables 92
potato-tomato soup with rosemary 51
ratatouille tart 81
spaghetti with arugula, tomato and avocado 62
stuffed pasta with feta, tomatoes and mint 60
tarte tatin provençal 85
tomato chutney 26
treacle tart 182
tuna: grilled niçoise salad 107
linguine with fresh tuna, puttanesca style 69
tuna in seaweed with pickled ginger sauce 109
Tunisian fish tagine 100
Tuscan salad 138

upside-down pear and raisin tart 183

vegetables: baby snapper on Thai curry
vegetables 102
baked vegetables with citrus 151
Brussels sprouts with walnuts, balsamic vinegar
and mint 147
couscous and vegetable stew 87
cream of roasted vegetable soup 46
gratin of eggplant with tomato and basil
vinaigrette 144
green herb pilaf 154
grilled vegetable lasagne 64
pakora with a spiced tomato chutney 26
parsley and grilled vegetable salad 135
polenta with grilled summer vegetables 92
pumpkin gratin 146
ratatouille tart 81
saffron couscous with spinach and red bell
pepper 155
spring vegetable soup 41
zucchinis with basil and Pecorino Romano
cheese 149
verjuice: salsa agresto 14
Vietnamese beef soup 44
Vietnamese minted lemon beef salad 130

walnuts: Brussels sprouts with walnuts, balsamic
vinegar and mint 147
eggplant and walnut rollups 27
salsa agresto 14
warm cappuccino bread pudding 174
warm potato and mussel salad 140
warm prawn and scallop salad with arugula 89
watercress: paillard of beef with watercress, olives
and tomatoes 118
white beans: rosemary-scented white bean
purée 13
white chocolate mousse with Frangelico 181
wild mushroom tart 79
wilted spinach salad with roasted bell pepper 132

yeasted apple tart 166
yogurt: minted yogurt sauce 24
zucchinis: zucchinis with basil and Pecorino
Romano cheese 149
parsley and grilled vegetable salad 135
polenta with grilled summer vegetables 92